The Butterfly Effect of Grace

Simple words.
Simple acts.
Simply amazing.

By Rex G. Russell

PRESS

table of contents

introductions

chapters

First,

I thank my God through

Jesus Christ

for

all

of

you.

romans 1:8
the amplified bible

Thank you.

I used to skip the thank you section of books I read. I just didn't get it. Why? Just tell your little world of supporters thank you and save the trees and ink. So why am I doing this thank you section? Because this is my first book and I had no idea how difficult it was. I have a friend who just published his first book and he told me it was the most physically draining thing he's ever done.

I get that.

When you and I look back over our lives, it seems like a marathon. Not a sprint. A marathon. Think of the people that have cheered you to keep running along the way or handed you water. For me this is thank you to the people that God placed in my life and sometimes in my way, that without them, I would have died of thirst. Some of them shoved gallons of water down my throat, some just quietly handed me a small cup and a nod. Even when I was in last place, they were there handing out encouragement, support, and a reason to keep going. When I could not take another step someone was cheering. I did want to quit, many times, but I kept running. Not a sprint, not even a jog sometimes. I just finished. Finishing is good. Over the past few months I have thought back over my life and began to picture the folks that have shaped my life and my heart. It humbles me. It really does. I know I would be a mess if God had not brought different people in my life, even though I didn't know at the time I needed them.

The first thank you is to a group of folks that God used to bridge me from brokenness. I had a tough experience on staff at a church. At the time I felt I had lost my voice and had nothing else to say. For someone who thought they had been called by God to speak His heart, I had no more words. I had convinced myself I was done, or better, God was done with me. I am not sure if I took a risk or if God pushed me off the diving board; but I jumped. I began to teach a small adult Bible study class on a Sunday morning. The first week we had 9 folks, counting myself and my wife, and a few couples we begged to show up. I am not sure why it never dawned on me, but this would be the first time in many, many years I would not be teaching students. I would be standing up in front of my peers, many of whom I had grown up with, teaching them each week. I really think if I had spent any time on that thought I would have backed out. Within a few weeks we had outgrown the little room we were in.

I remember telling a close friend I had decided to use a very simple teaching format. I would stand up each week and tell them what it seemed God had done in my life and how I was going to try and make it to the next week. I would be very transparent, and I would be brutally honest about where I was. One morning a woman in the class walked up to me after I had taught and asked me a question. She said to me, "Were you serious about what you said this morning?" I laughed and told her I said a lot, and wanted to know which part she was questioning. She said, "You said you struggle every day to have a consistent walk with God." I told her I was very serious. She told me she thought she was the only one.

She thought she was the only one.

The only one.

That afternoon I went home and wrote this sentence in my journal,

"Nothing I will ever do,
good or bad,
will ever cause the heart of God
to love me any more
or less
than He does
right
now."

Even as I write that sentence, I hear myself saying that over, and over, and over again in front of folks over the past few years. I said it sometimes just to see the look on their face. I wanted to see if they received that radical idea or if they recoiled because that sounded too risky.

Risky for who? Them or God?

Whose reputation was at risk?

That became the defining phrase for me, and I think for that class. It seemed to clarify what had been foggy. I know it mowed down some religious theology that had lots of folks tied up. From that point forward I told that group of adults that God loved them, and they could stop running from or to God. Just stand still and know that He is all you will ever need. That class, over the next six years, reshaped what God was doing in my life. As much as they might have thought I was teaching them, they taught me. It was the most rewarding and fulfilling time in my ministry life. I saw the light come on in the eyes and hearts of so many folks. I refused to give them a list of rules. I wanted them to know that God loved them unconditionally.

Really.

I knew that for many of them it would be the first time they heard that message.

Maybe the only time.

So to that group of folks who sat under my teaching for those six years, thank you. You have no idea how many kind words you shared with me, that carried me through some very challenging times. Sometimes when you thought I was up there handing out sage wisdom, I was really wondering if any of this made sense, or if it would ever cause anyone to connect the dots to God. I hope it did. I have said for years that you teach to faces and eyes. You lean into those who seem to be connecting with what is coming out of your heart. To this day, I look back on some of those mornings when I just was not sure if anything I was saying was landing, and I would catch a certain look. You encouraged me to continue, week after week with your learning, listening heart. Leaving that class to plant a church was a very difficult decision. Hardest we have ever made. It was the right decision, but I did not want to leave that family. Your faith was contagious.

To Justin & Wendi Zebell. You make it difficult to answer the question, "How many kids do you guys have?" You know how we feel about you both. Justin, words cannot express how proud I am of you. From the time I first met you as a skinny, goofy, clumsy, 7th grader, you have captured my heart. Your father's day card to me is always a highlight of my year. I now understand you were one of the main reasons I came to that church. You are a good son; you need to know that. I will spend the rest of my life praying for you and Wendi and the children that will grow up in your home. You have come light years from the original 'my bad' that night in the MPR. Just think, now you are on speed dial with most of Nashville and the world! By the way, the Eskimos are still buying ice aren't they? You learn well grass hopper.

To David & Jean Young. I could not have asked for better in-laws. David you have fixed enough broken things at your daughter's house over the years to empty a Home Depot. Thank you. How did you ever get a son-in-law that doesn't know a crescent wrench from a croissant sandwich? That had to be your worst nightmare! Jean, thank you for raising the little girl that I would spend the rest of my life with. You taught her how to create the most incredible home, where people find a safe place to land. You and David both are the joy of Jeanene's life. I understand the definition of love when I watch her care for both you. I just wish you would have taught her that cats are evil and must be avoided at all cost. We have four. That is five too many. I am learning to love cats. We have a cat named Dawg. That helps.

To Mike & Janet. I love the life we share. Some of our safest, let your hair down, moments are with you guys. Your support in this church plant has been an anchor. Watching our boys grow up together, more as brothers than cousins, has been a blessing.

To George & Melodi. You too, are the reason we consider our life to be abundant. It matters that you know how much I value the late night phone calls and how much I feel safe dumping and venting when life gets tangled. Those three nieces fill a significant void in my life; I get to watch Jeanene 'raise', even from a distance, the little girls she never had.

To my Mom and Dad. You need to know how much I love and appreciate you both. Now that I have a twenty-two year old college graduate, I am amazed at how much I took for granted. You sacrificed to give your kids more than they deserved; I now understand that. The older I get the more I look back and love the memories I have growing up in our home. I especially think of you every time someone says, "We had a dog named Rex."

To my son Dawson. I always wondered what my dad was thinking when he watched me growing up. What went through his mind as he saw me in sports, in school, in life? What was he thinking when he saw me leave for college and begin my life? I now know. He almost could not contain the joy and pride. Before you could form your first word, God taught me volumes about himself through you. Quite simply, you changed my life forever. I am amazed at how God has used you to display his Grace through your design work. I genuinely believe, at times, God has given you the ability to translate His heart. Your creative design work on this book has meant the world to me. You have such an incredible life before you; live it to the fullest.

To my wife Jeanene. I have told people for years, much to your chagrin, that I married Ellie May Clampet. You do have your cement pond and critters. Lord knows how many 'strays' we have taken in, cleaned up, hauled to the vet, named, and then years later buried. There is a patch of our land that is Steven King's 'Pet Cemetery'. But that is such a picture of your life. Over the years you have taken in 'stray' seminary and college students, broke ministry couples, cooked hundreds of meals, and hosted huge cookouts and outdoor gatherings. I remember when we counted 127 people, with Mechele raking grass out of the house. How many Friday and Saturday nights did you cook for 30, 40, or 50 'stray' high school kids like ants on chocolate. Or the time I found you crying in the bathroom after counseling two young girls from their brokenness and pain. Is it any wonder that your calling in life was to work with special education students? You find ways to celebrate a high school diploma as if it is a Nobel Peace Prize; because in many ways to you, it is. Again, when someone drops off a stray, you just cannot help yourself. You mend wounds and untangle knots. You were wired by God to bring the hurting and helpless inside. Your heart and home have become a safe refuge. Everyone who has eaten a meal, stayed a night, or moved in for a while, knows this to be so true. Your life embodies the title of this book. Thank you for letting me love you for the rest of your life.

foreword.

Rex Russell is a great story teller. He always has been. He looks at the tiny details of life and finds the simple meanings most of us miss. And he brings those meanings to life through his stories. It is a gift. Until now I've only heard him tell these stories. I'm glad he's decided to share some of them in this book.

Many people could share stories of how the grace of God has changed their lives. Rex is no exception. His life has been changed by grace. In *the butterfly effect of grace*, he gives a unique look at how you and I can respond to and share grace with others. He shares this with conviction because he lives it. It's more than just words for Rex. I know that because God used Rex to show His grace to me.

I met Rex in 1990 at a Disciple-Now weekend in Quero, Texas, where he was the weekend speaker. I was a college student and small group leader who had no idea what I was doing there. Really. I was coming out of a life-changing injury as a college athlete. I knew I was searching, but I was in no way a leader. God spoke to me that weekend through what Rex said, and I began thinking about what could be. I started catching on to this idea of grace, that God could use me in spite of me.

Several weeks passed. I felt a connection to Rex and decided to call him and ask his advice on God's calling in my life. He listened. I started calling him several times a week. We would talk for an hour, sometimes two. Soon, I knew his number by heart. You get the picture: a needy college kid searching for God's will, contemplating God's call on my life, and needing to talk to someone, even someone I had only known for two days.

What was the draw?

I saw God's grace in Rex's life, and I wanted to know more. He could have changed his number, or he could have asked his wife to say he wasn't home. He could have told me to quit calling and get a life. He didn't. He listened. He was gracious. I am so grateful!

As you read this book, you'll realize that Rex loves to collide with people who are disconnected with the heart of God, and offer them a life of hope. A life that is full of grace. Not so they can sit and stare at their own life, but so they can be inspired to give away what they now have. That kind of grace really is amazing!

You may never get the chance to sit down with Rex like I have, but sit down with this book, and you'll feel like you're with him. As you read his stories of God's grace, I pray that your eyes will be opened, like mine have, to see the effects of God's grace and mercy all around you.

Bubba Thurman
Pastor - Lake Pointe Church
Rockwall, Texas

"Chaos often breeds life,
when
order
breeds
habit."
-Henry Adams

We are therefore Christ's ambassadors,
as though God were making his appeal
through
us.
We implore you on Christ's behalf:
Be
reconciled
to
God.
2 Corinthians 5:19-20 NIV

preface.

Welcome. First, thank you for taking time to read this book. It is humbling you would carve out time to read what's written on these pages. You have lots of choices of what to do with your time and most of us have very little to spare; thank you. Second, I need you to know I wrote this book for those of us that need to be reminded our life matters. The things we do and say matter. It matters to God, and it matters to those around you. That is the central message of this book. I hope that resonates with you. And finally, I want to tell you that *the butterfly effect of grace* is a collection of stories I have either personally experienced or have been told firsthand. When I used names and specific details, I have asked, and I have been given permission to share their story.

It matters that you know that as well.

Some of the stories in this book are very personal and entail very detailed accounts of their life. There are pages in this book that seem so hopeless and dark. Keep reading. For every shade of pain, there is a shade of grace. God works His purpose in the end. Remember, everything is connected. Everything tends to make more sense, if we keep that in mind. God does not cause all things, but He causes all things to work together for the good. Get to the good.

The idea for this book did not come from any great single revelation. There was not one moment when it all came rushing in. I really believe it came from random observations over time. I have for years wondered if anyone noticed that it seems God does His most amazing work through the lives of simple, almost insignificant people. Look at the New Testament—the woman at the well, the woman caught in adultery, the thief on the cross, Zacchaeus, on and on. The Old Testament is full of obscure, sometimes even odd people and events that link together a story of God drawing His children back to Himself. From the opening of Genesis to the end of Revelation, God seems to blow the wind of heaven through people we know almost nothing about and for the most part never hear from again.

But He does His work through them.
And it is good.

It is very good.

For example, the only reason you and I know about Mother Teresa is because she lived in an age when she was filmed and photographed, making a public record of her life. I'm sure it would have been fine with her if she had lived and done her work two hundred years ago when no one but the children and poor she worked with would have known her. I never met Mother Teresa, but I can almost assure you she never wanted any of the praise, recognition, or notoriety she received. It surely was never her goal to be famous. She wanted to make the mercy of God famous. She was buried with all her worldly possessions: her comb and toothbrush. We know that because—without her permission and probably to her dismay—we laid her in a glass case on view for days.

Many times when Jesus healed someone, He sent them away with a command like "Don't tell anyone about this!"

Why? He knew the crowds would follow the miracles and miss the Messiah.

He was so right.
We still do that today.

Yes we do.

Think about the simple ways God seems to move through the lives of each of us to call His children back to Himself. He seems to use small, almost invisible events and people to cover the world with His finger prints.

Look at the words of II Chronicles 16:9 from the New American Standard:

"For the eyes of the LORD move to and fro throughout the earth that He may strongly support those whose heart is completely His."

What does that mean? I can't say I know everything the verse implies, but I do know it moves me. It motivates me to get in the game and to take a risk to connect with folks who are hurting and seem empty. It encourages me that when I do, I am not alone; God is in the middle of that effort. That is such an empowering truth for you and I.

the butterfly effect of grace.

Odd title? I remember when I first began to think through the idea of that title. It seemed I'd had a front row seat to some amazing events, and the privilege of meeting some incredible people. "the butterfly effect of grace" seemed to describe what I was feeling as I thought through these stories.

What exactly does "the butterfly effect of grace" mean? First, the butterfly effect comes from a peculiar place. It is a reference from the Chaos Theory of Mathematics. It is a phrase that describes what could happen if a butterfly were simply to brush its wings against the air, a few inches just above the ocean water, eventually creating an enormous tidal wave.

The original Butterfly Effect theory is attributed to Professor Edward Lorenz. In a 1963 paper given to the New York Academy of Sciences he wrote:

"One meteorologist remarked that if the theory were correct, one flap of a seagull's wings would be enough to alter the course of the weather forever."

At the December 1972 convention of the American Association for the Advancement of Science in Washington, D.C., the sea gull seemed to morph into a butterfly. The title of his talk was: *Predictability: Does the Flap of a Butterfly's Wings in Brazil set off a Tornado in Texas?*

One writer says it this way:

"The butterfly effect states that if a butterfly were to flap its wings at just the right time, at precisely the right place over the ocean, it would start a tidal wave off the coast of China that would cause a hurricane in Texas."

Wow.

Can you picture that? A tiny butterfly somewhere off the coast of China, doing the simplest thing it was created to do, suddenly causes a ripple effect flooding the other side of the world.

Stop and think about that.

The butterfly doesn't set out to change the world or even cause a flood; it just flaps its wings. The butterfly doesn't make a sound. You have never 'heard' a butterfly do anything. It is silent. How powerful is the common butterfly? The average butterfly only lives for two to four weeks. The longest any known butterfly species lives is nine months. A full-grown butterfly weighs no more than two grams, the same as a spoonful of salt.

A full-grown butterfly has no business flying out over the ocean.

It's much too dangerous, the risk is too great.

The result of one tiny wave could be tragic: no more butterfly. Yet butterflies have been found on remote islands where they are not native and some have been found in the middle of the ocean on oil rigs.

On oil rigs?

What can you and I learn from this?

The seemingly insignificant encounters we have every day *do matter*. What we say, how we respond, when we encourage someone, and who we connect with matter tremendously. Nothing we do this side of heaven is coincidental. Through the eyes of God nothing is an accident, and nothing is an incident. Is it possible that the simple, silent, almost invisible life of a butterfly is God's way of proving that?

You and I are part of a plan. His plan. This is not a cosmic chess game. This is the sovereign loving plan for God Himself to reconnect with His children, *through His children*. When you have the opportunity to flap your own butterfly wings, do it. You never know when it might move the ocean of someone's life.

Grace.

So many images pop up in my mind when I think of the word grace. I had heard the word countless times during my life, but I didn't really think it through until 1988. That was the year Chuck Swindoll came out with the book *The Grace Awakening*. I read that book from cover to cover in about a week. For someone with incurable ADD, that's not bad. I felt like I was reading my own thoughts on paper— that this life was intended to be lived in total freedom, liberty, and joy (not fear, anger, or worry). When Paul said, "It is for freedom that you have been set free," He meant just that. In John 10:10 He said, "I have come that they would have life and that they would live it to the fullest."

Grace is the meteor that hit this planet two thousand years ago when Jesus came to earth as a human. He was God incarnate, God wrapped in the skin and bone of man. He was as much God as if He was not man at all. He was as much man as if He was not God at all. He wasn't fifty/fifty; He was 100 percent God and 100 percent man. That is the only way you can ever understand and explain how He could hurt, bleed, cry out, die, *and* save my soul all at the same time. And all of that was done through grace.

When you allow grace to soak in, it liberates you from trying to fix others. It frees you to just love them, all the way through, to the bone. It liberates you from trying to fix yourself too. You don't have a license to sin, but you have the option to forgive—to forgive yourself and to love yourself. Remember what Jesus said? "Love your neighbor *as you love yourself.*" Is it possible that I don't or can't love my neighbor because I really don't love, forgive, accept, and believe myself? When the concept and reality of grace drips down into my heart, the only way I can respond to myself and to the rest of the world is with love. Love God, love yourself, and love the people around you. No more complicated than that.

Grace is in short supply. Most people feel certain that grace applies to them, and they are ok with it landing on other folks too, as long as they aren't *too* bad. The truth is that your sin and my sin crucified the only Son of God. You and I were responsible. We didn't drive the nails, but our sin planned every moment of that day. We were the reason that day occurred. The heart of God broke because my broken life took the breath from Christ. His heart stopped beating because mine was wicked. God the Father not only forgave you, but He adopted you as His child and moved you into His home. You are not an ignored neighbor who is stared at through the window. You sit at His dinner table and you live and you laugh and you have your very being because of Him.

Because grace is true, you have a story to tell. You have a reason to embrace and hand out grace. It is the only reason you draw a breath. It was the process that rushed you back into the very presence of God. You walk in through the front door, and you are greeted as a prince in from battle. You are welcome in your Father's house.

You have a name. You have your own room and you have every reason to believe that your best days are ahead of you. Grace bought you and freed you, and today it holds you up and places one of your feet in front of the other. It is not the main thing; it is the only thing. If you remove grace from the mind and heart of God, you dissolve this universe instantly. There is no reason for one grain of dust to remain if He is not viewing you and me through the eyes of grace.

What happens when you and I wrap our minds and our hands around this truth? It causes a butterfly effect. It creates ripples and waves that will cover and flood everything—from the simplest and tiniest people, places, and causes to the largest and most significant. The most important thing about the butterfly effect of grace is that it starts when you and I simply open our eyes and notice the world around us. It is about God using us to reach out to hurting people. It is about helping them connect the dots back to God because you took the risk to flap your wings one more time.

My prayer for this book is that you will be inspired, that you will be encouraged, and that you will see there really are no insignificant words, actions, prayers, or people in the Kingdom of God. I pray that somehow you will step out, take a risk, and cause a butterfly effect of grace.

rest in Him,
rex

The mass of men lead lives
of
quiet
desperation.
-Henry David Thoreau

Quietly trust yourself to Christ your Lord,
and if anybody asks why you believe as
you do,
be ready to tell him,
and do it
in a gentle
and
respectful way.
1 Peter 3:15 TLB

blue jeans, sandals, and the hard rock hotel.

It was the first leg of my flight home. I was leaving Minneapolis with a connection in Cincinnati, then to Dallas, before a forty-minute drive home. I had been on the road for a few days and I was really tired and *really* ready to get home.

I had a new copy of *The Message Remix* and wanted to read through some of Psalms for a while. This flight was at night; it was quiet and dark, just a small overhead reading light above me. The flight was so smooth I almost forgot I was sitting on a plane. I had only been reading a few minutes when the lady sitting across the aisle leaned over and said,

"Sir, could I borrow a pen?"

I handed her a pen and she said, "Thank you, sir." A few moments later she dropped the pen and I reached down and handed it to her.

"Thank you, sir."

Odd. I'm in my mid-forties but have lots of grey hair (think Taylor Hicks, 2006 American Idol winner) and I remember thinking, "Ok, enough with the 'sir.'" She and I looked to be about the same age and I thought it was funny she was addressing me as if I was twice her age. Just before we began our descent, she handed me the pen and quietly said,

"Thank you, sir, for letting me use your pen, sir."

I was amused at this point. I felt like Grandpa on *The Waltons*. My gosh, how old do I look? We deplaned and everyone scattered. My layover in Cincinnati was only forty-five minutes, which gave me time to grab a quick burger and catch the last leg to Dallas. Finally headed home. I was leaning on a rail outside McDonald's when I looked up and noticed the same lady who had borrowed my pen on the plane. She was walking right toward me. I had already decided if she asked me for the pen I was going to give the pen to her and not take any chances of being called "sir" anymore! She walked right up to me with a very cautious but determined and desperate look on her face and carefully said to me,

"Sir, are you from Cincinnati?"

I must confess I was worried where this line of questioning was headed. Before I could answer, she said,

"You *are* a priest, aren't you?"

A little background.

That morning I had thrown on a pair of pressed blue jeans, open-toed sandals, and an untucked black, open collar Hard Rock Hotel button-up shirt—You know, the cool-looking shirt that makes middle-aged guys feel, well, cool. I also had on my trademark white undershirt t-shirt that I wear no matter how cold or hot it is, underneath the Hard Rock shirt. Not the sleeveless tank top style; just a white t-shirt. Like the guys in the movie *Grease* wore. Try it. It works.

So here I was wearing a black, open-collar, button-up shirt with a white t-shirt showing just a bit above the top button. Got the picture?

When I realized what—or better, who—she thought I was, I laughed and said, "No I am not a priest. Besides, I don't think most priests would be wearing blue jeans, sandals, and a Hard Rock Hotel shirt, would they?" To which she said with much disappointment in her eyes,

"Well, I was hoping so. When I saw you getting on the plane and then I saw you reading the scriptures, I hoped you were a priest here in Cincinnati. I told myself if you *were* a priest and you had a Catholic church in this area and you were that comfortable wearing that shirt, well, I had decided I was going to go to your church because I haven't been in years. Thank you, sir."

And with that she walked off.

I am never without words. This time I could not say a thing. She was gone around the corner before I could gather any thoughts of what had just happened. I sat down. My mind raced back to the plane ride. What must she have been thinking when she thought I was a local Catholic priest, brave enough to wear blue jeans, sandals, and a stupid Hard Rock shirt, but comfortable enough to read a Bible sitting on an airplane? What was it like in her mind when she tried to get up the courage to walk over to me, a priest, and find out where the 'others' were meeting?

Where did she go after she found out I wasn't a priest? Why did she keep referring to me as 'Sir' and not the traditional 'Father' if she thought I was a priest? What did she think while she was driving home? Did she cry? Did she wonder what I must be thinking? Was she embarrassed? Did she drive right to the first Catholic church and sit down and pray or talk to someone? Where is she today? What is she doing right now? Is she reading this sentence? Does she ever think about that day?

I do.

All the time.

I wonder what might have happened if I had been able to sit down and talk to her, even for ten minutes. What if she had given me her e-mail address and I was able to find her a great local church, Catholic or not, and helped her get plugged back into something? I don't say that to beat myself up. I say it just for this point: How many random moments do you and I miss every day? Who is watching you right now thinking, "If they'll just leave a bread trail, I'll follow them out of this dark cave." Who is sitting in an airport right now looking around for someone to make sense of this crazy fallen world?

This reminded me of a scene I witnessed not long ago, in another airport. We were delayed and the flights just before ours were delayed as well. You may have seen this before. The waiting area is packed and people are standing talking on the phone, or asking the poor lady at the desk how much longer. Everyone is frustrated or worried and every person has a story why they have to be in the next open seat. There I was with nothing to do but wait. A young woman sitting in the same uncomfortable chairs I was in answered a cell phone call. It was obvious this was a call she had been waiting for. Not in a good way either. Her boyfriend, we all found out at very high decibels, was the one responsible for booking this trip.

Evidently he was also the cause of the plane delay, global warming, and world hunger. This guy was in hot water. I honestly don't know if he got a word in edgewise. She lit him up for a good twenty minutes. Toward the end of the call she began to use horrible language. People started getting up and moving away from her as if she were throwing darts. It was amazing. I could only stare in disbelief. Women, children, me, and everyone else in that cubby hole heard this onslaught. She got louder and angrier. I really thought someone was going to come up and ask her to stop or leave. They didn't and neither did she.

To be honest, I normally would have been the one that stepped in to tell her to shut up. This time it seemed like I was supposed to sit and listen—not to the beating she was dishing out or the foul language we were all being subjected to, but it seemed I was supposed to listen to something else. I began to ask this question:

"Who broke your heart?"

I didn't say it to her; I just kept asking myself. This was not about the guy on the other end of the call; this was about a little girl who had gotten crushed at some point. She was mad at the world and this poor guy was in the wrong place at the right time. I got a picture in my mind of a girl whose heart was burned badly by someone she trusted. Physical, emotional, psychological, it doesn't matter. Someone at some point stepped into her world and tore out her heart. She was going to get back at the world, one train wreck at a time. I tried to imagine her getting married, only to destroy one relationship after another. I will never forget watching her going at this guy on the phone. I so wanted to have a Dr. Phil moment with her and walk over and take the phone out of her hand, hang it up, and look at her and say,

"How's this working for you?"

I doubt she would have been able to answer that question. Isn't it amazing how simple the answers to life seem to be when you watch others spin out of control? Maybe that could be the beginning of wisdom, to be able to see yourself as others see you.

Maybe?

I think about that encounter on the plane that night. I wonder what might have happened if the lady on the plane would have leaned over to me during the flight and asked me if I was a priest. What if I told her I was not a priest, but I would do my best to listen? What if I had asked her,

"Why do you ask?"

What would she have said?

Think about it. She would have said something, right? For her to find me in the airport and walk up and ask that question, something was on her heart. Can you imagine what we might have talked about on that quiet plane ride into Cincinnati that night? If she grew up Catholic, maybe the idea of a priest opened her heart to the need to talk to someone right there about something. Maybe she needed to confess something. Maybe just the thought of seeing a priest sitting across the aisle gave her courage to reach out that night. I have no idea. Something was going on in her heart; that I am sure of.

I do think about that day a lot. I wonder about the lady that borrowed my pen and sat there while I was reading Psalms. Maybe after she shared with me what was on her mind, I could have turned over to the forty-second chapter of Psalms, verse 11:

"Why am I discouraged? Why so sad? I will put my hope in God! I will praise him again—my Savior and my God!"

Maybe that would have connected the dots. Maybe.

P.S. If you are a Catholic Priest in the Cincinnati area, I dare you to wear blue jeans, open-toed sandals, and a black Hard Rock Hotel shirt tomorrow; there's a lady in your town looking for you. Lead her back home. The white t-shirt is optional.

If you live in Cincinnati and you somehow know this lady I met on the plane, call her today. Buy her a cup of coffee for me and listen to her and make sure she understands God has loved her every day of her life. He has never left her. Especially when she felt the most alone. If you don't know her, take someone else. Anyone. Listen to their story. Tell them God is standing in their tomorrow; their best days are ahead of them.

If you are that lady in the plane that day, I am so sorry I just stood there and said nothing. You stumped me. Like I told you, I wasn't a Catholic priest. I didn't know what to say. I didn't know any churches in the area. I didn't grow up Catholic like you, but I did grow up needing to know that God desperately loves me. *That*, I could have and should have shared with you. I think that was really what you were asking for that day. Not a pen. Sometimes now when I'm sitting on a plane waiting for it to take off or land, I pray that the person sitting next me encounters God in a way that changes them forever. I pray for you too. Please pray for me. Thank you for gathering the courage to walk over and ask that seemingly random question. Just in case you wondered if God could ever use you, He just did.

The answer to the question that seemed to be in your eyes is this:

Yes, you are forgiven,
and yes,
you are free;
because of what Christ did for you.

Nothing you will ever do or ever have done, good or bad, will ever cause the heart of God to love you any more or less than He does right now; you don't have to run to or from Him; just stand still.

You are safe there.

Bless you, lady.
E-mail me; I found a church for you in Cincinnati.

If you want to build a ship,
don't herd people together to collect
wood
and don't assign them tasks and work,
but rather teach them to long for the
endless
immensity
of the
sea.
antoine de saint-exupery

'Go quickly into the streets and alleys
of the city and invite the poor, the
crippled, the lame, and the blind.' After
the servant had done this, he reported,
'There is still room for more.' So his
master said, 'Go out into the country
lanes and behind the hedges and urge
anyone you find to come, so that the
house will be full.'
Luke 14:21-24 NLT

dirt and dogs welcome.

I remember when a buddy of mine first told me this story.
We were sitting in an IHOP eating waffles with that IHOP
butter (blended with honey, sugar, and raw cholesterol),
whipped cream, and tons of syrup. You can just hear our
arteries hardening right now, can't you?

My friend's uncle was the pastor of a large church in the
Midwest. Weeks before this, a tornado ripped through their
community one night, leveling many homes and buildings.
Minutes after the devastating winds and rain blew through,
survivors began walking through the rubble to find
what was left and who was still alive. As local radio and
television stations regained their signals, word got out that
the Red Cross had set up a "command central" and shelter
at this large church. There they would begin the process
of medical assessment, the distribution of food, water, and
blankets, and most importantly, the sorting out of those
who were still lost and unaccounted for.

Red Cross volunteers manned every entrance to the
church building. As folks wandered up to the volunteers'
tables, triage determined what was needed. They also
gathered basic information—name, address, phone
numbers, next of kin—to determine who was still missing.

The pastor noticed as he walked around the church halls,
offices, and meeting rooms that there was a very distinct
look to the people there. They were covered in mud from
head to toe. No one escaped the mess left by the storm.
Making their way to this Red Cross makeshift "MASH"
unit was no easy task. Folks had to climb, dig, slip, and
slide their way to the safe refuge of this well-known church

building. Within a few minutes the church became a complete wreck. Carpet and walls, chairs and stairs were covered in mud and trash. It was futile to attempt to "wipe your feet off." There was nothing clean to use. The entire area was a mud pit.

One other thing was strikingly different about this midnight "congregation": They brought their cats and dogs.

Think about it.

If you flee a destroyed home and run to shelter, you grab your pets. You snatch up cats and dogs and head to dry, safe ground. So, much to the delight of this pastor and his staff, in spite of the night's sudden events, the church building was full of frightened, cold, and wet townspeople who had found their way inside a place of refuge. They were being loved on, cared for, treated, warmed, and welcomed. Somehow it just felt right, on a night when so much had gone terribly wrong. You can only imagine what it must have looked like inside this beautiful church building as the night unfolded with hundreds of hurting, filthy, and scared people with lots and lots of cats and dogs running and barking. There had to be at least one dog that thought, "I have died and gone to heaven! I must have. I'm in a church, and it is full of cats! They can't get out, so I will chase them for all eternity! This IS heaven!"

In an effort to help at the Red Cross registration tables, some of the church support staff were categorizing registration cards, to better determine who was okay and who was still missing. At one point, an associate pastor approached the senior pastor and informed him that something odd was occurring. After looking through the hundreds of information cards, it was becoming clear that most, if not all, of these folks lived within a few blocks of the church property but almost none of them were church members. In fact, most of them were not members of any local church, though they obviously lived within walking distance of a very good local community church.

The associate pastor said, "I don't understand; how did we miss these people? They live right in our back yard, yet I have never seen them until tonight."

Looking over the huge crowd of people and animals, the pastor simply said,

"Until tonight, they knew their dirt and dogs were not welcome."

Obviously he was not referring to the mutts and mud. He was making a much larger observation. He was saying that somehow "we" have given subtle, but strong signals that you need to clean up and straighten up if you want to join our club. We didn't print the message on a sign or a banner or in an ad in the local newspaper. No guards stood at the entry doors to our churches. No pamphlets were passed out in the neighborhoods. No, it was much louder and clearer than that. Over the past few decades we have so organized, structured, and strategized the New Testament church that it no longer feels welcoming to the very people it was created to reach: sheep who are lost from the fold.

We have become the hospital that truly prefers its patients get well before they are allowed to see the doctor. When did the change happen? Was there a day when some guy stood up and said, "I'm pretty much done with this reach-the-world game plan. Can we just focus on us for a while?

Let's build large buildings and buy lots and lots of property, and in the process go into such crippling debt we will ensure we never see the light of day"?

Did it happen that way? Did that guy sit down and then the entire group look at each other and agree that was a good plan? Did we one day just abandon the simple, clear mandate handed down by Christ: to make disciples, baptize them, teach them how to do the same thing, and then keep doing it until the world is reached?

No, it didn't happen on one day. Instead, we slowly grew away from the simple process of eating in each other's homes, selling what we had, and growing in love toward each other and the Lord. Church historians tell us the first century church was referred to as "The Way." Go figure. Jesus said: "I am the way, the truth, and the life. No man comes unto the Father except through Me."

When did we install "the system" in place of "the way"?

The book of Acts says that in the early days Christians would get together every day to pray, fellowship, eat, and listen to the apostles. Read Acts 2:42-47. When was the first time someone realized we missed yesterday? Who made mention it had been a few days since we sat under the teaching of the apostles? Who was the first person to say, "Is it just me, or has it been two weeks since we ate together and prayed?"

When did it become commonplace to be, well, common?

Was it six months? Within the first year? Who quit first? Who was the first one that walked away from The Way? Were they still meeting in huddled masses in their homes when someone suddenly looked up and said, "What's today? It's been a year. One year ago today I watched Him die. I can't believe it."

Did anyone notice?

We have come full circle. Read the last few chapters of each of the Gospels, and then finish the first two or three chapters of Acts. Notice the flow of people? Seamless? Almost a reckless abandon of what was safe.

If the western church is ever going to regain its relevance, it has got to acknowledge that folks do have a choice. They can walk past our steeples, shake their heads, and never look back. I have heard preachers state for years that the church is "not about you," meaning that the sole purpose of the church is to reach the lost.

Wrong.

The sole purpose of the New Testament church is to teach, train, encourage, educate, inspire, and involve the believer to live life to the fullest—the abundant life. That is how you make disciples. You can't make disciples unless someone becomes a believer, a Christ follower. If my life is ever going to be an appealing option to a disconnected, confused, lost world, it has got to be different; it has got to be full of life, and it has got to offer hope in a terribly hopeless world! If my day-to-day life demonstrates hope, joy, and peace in a chaotic, hurried, indifferent world, someone will notice the difference. And the only source of that difference is Christ.

John Piper said it best:

"The purpose of the church is not missions. The purpose of the church is worship. The purpose of missions is to bring more worshipers to the kingdom of God."

I still believe folks will pull up lawn chairs for days and days to hear there is something beyond themselves, something better than just marking time and waiting to die. When the message of my life is real, it is contagious. When that happens, the world will find its way into our lives and into our churches—not into our church buildings necessarily, but into our churches. The most powerful marketing plan for the church is changed lives without any gimmicks. And the only way for real change to take place is an encounter with Christ.

When you and I live out our faith in a choppy, painful world where folks get sick, lose their jobs, get divorced, fight addictions, and sometimes never win and eventually die, we will at the very least cause the world to wonder what the difference is. It is at that point we tell them our stories of how Grace found and rescued us.

Michael Wells of Abiding Life Ministries says it this way: "The measure of a man's faith is not how much he can receive, but how long he will remain faithful when he receives nothing."

Wow. I would want to know the source of that person's faith. Wouldn't you?

I want others to see something in my day-to-day life that makes them stop and ask. It is at that point the perfect storm builds and dialogue begins. We start to communicate, and before you know it, a connection is made and a question is asked, and maybe it's answered.

If not, someone talked and someone listened. They'll be back. If it's real, they'll be back. Notice how Jesus connected with the world he walked in; dialogue. He sat and talked to hurting, curious folks. He answered their questions and He gave them hope. Sometimes His answers were tough. But, He reached inside and healed their wounded heart. Why do we think we have to come up with a better method?

We must start today rebuilding the bridge that allows folks to visit and "window shop" at their own heart's pace. The church has got to start looking, sounding, and feeling more like a teaching hospital and less like a lake lot tour. Let that soak in. Those two scenarios are vastly different, and they treat people very differently.

God is not in a hurry.

Even if we are behind on budget, He is not in a hurry.

He knows the name of the last person who will walk into heaven and the name of the last person who won't. We have turned the spirit of God into an impatient, upset, sometimes angry and frustrated warden who will put us all in lock down or solitary if we don't act better.

Lost people act like lost people.

They do things that lost people do. Some of them act good, some of them act bad, but at the end of the day they act lost. God knows that. He's not nervous or surprised. He has a plan.

He is very okay with their dirt and their dogs.

When did you and I become so uncomfortable with their dirt and their dogs?

When did you and I forget we once were covered in mud?

If you claim to be a believer and a follower of the life and teachings of Christ, at one point you stumbled inside, cold and wet, with your dirt and your dog. You were helped inside and given a blanket and a warm cup of coffee. Someone explained to you that even though you were lost and confused, you were safe now.

Look out the stained glass windows of your church. People are standing out in the rain, covered in mud. A tornado has ripped their lives apart and they are scared to death. If you and I don't do something soon, they'll just keep walking. God knows where they'll end up.

God knows where they'll end up.

Open the door.
Let them in.
Don't worry about the paw prints.

All dogs go to heaven.

Millions long for immortality
who don't know what to do with
themselves
on a rainy
Sunday
afternoon.
-Susan Ertz

The next day John saw Jesus coming
toward him, and said, "Behold! The
Lamb of God who takes away the sin of
the world!
John 1:29 NKJV

cappuccinos and tattoos.

It was a Saturday afternoon. I will never ever forget
that day. We owned a small coffee house next to the
convention center and we had been busy all day. I walked
into Kinko's to print something when I overheard someone
on a cell phone:

"How is he? Did he sleep any? Did you? I'll be there in
about twenty minutes; you can get some rest. I'll sit with
him tonight. Want some coffee? I'll look for a Starbucks."

When he hung up I asked if he needed a coffee house. He
asked if I knew where the closest Starbucks was. I pointed
across the street and told him I owned that little coffee
house. I told him we were closed, but an employee was
cleaning up and would wait for us. He thanked me and said
that would be great. I told him I couldn't help but overhear
him, and asked if someone was in the hospital. He told me
no. He said he had just placed his thirty-two-year-old son
in hospice with cancer.

Thirty-two years old.

We began to talk and he told me he was from California.
He and his other son, Scott, were here now in Texas
staying around the clock at hospice. He told me his name
was Don and his son who was sick was Chad. A few years
ago Chad noticed a small black mole on his arm. It ended
up being one of the most aggressive forms of melanoma.
By this time, the cancer was very advanced and the family
had decided to place Chad in the care of a local hospice
service.

Don was at Kinko's to laminate a poster. The poster had pictures of Chad and the Dallas Mavericks basketball team, with many of the players, head coach Avery Johnson, and owner Mark Cuban. Chad was an incredible basketball player. He was an all star in high school, setting the scoring record for that school. When he moved to Dallas he went on to become the 1999 international 'Hoop Shoot' champion, making Chad the best in the world at free throws and three-point shots. Just before he was diagnosed with cancer, he was slated to play professional basketball in Europe. Chad was usually the best player on the court. Any court, anywhere in the world. While living in Dallas he made a connection with the Dallas Mavericks. The Mavericks had a 'Chad Matz' night, where they honored Chad in front of the entire crowd.

It would be his last game to watch.

One picture on the poster seemed very unique: Chad was sitting in a wheelchair, patch over one eye, very weak from the final stages of cancer, with Mark Cuban leaning down. Chad had pulled Cuban down to him, and he was whispering something into Mark's ear. You could see that Mark Cuban was obviously listening very carefully.

Chad was praying for Mark.

Don said Mark Cuban walked away with tears in his eyes. The Mavericks lost the game that night. Cuban came over to Chad afterwards and apologized for the loss.

Don and I walked across the street to get coffee so he could relieve Scott who was sitting with Chad. Just before Don left, I asked if we could pray for him and his boys. He sat down and we prayed. At the end of the prayer, Don began to weep. It was an exhausted, worn out cry. It was a cry that only a father knows. It is the kind of cry that comes from a broken heart. This father wanted to pick his son up and wipe the blood off of his scraped knee. Don cried because he had to watch as the knee bled and bled and bled. It was a cry of helplessness. Not hopelessness, but helplessness. There is a big difference.

As he was leaving the coffee house, Don said to Shawn, "Would you visit Chad? He would like that very much." Shawn was a great kid. Long blond pony tail, torn blue jeans, and a heart for Jesus. He was a street preacher and musician. He went that day and visited Chad. Chad was not feeling well at all, but when Shawn walked in his room Chad suddenly became alert and awake, and sat up in bed and talked to Shawn for over an hour. He said it just flowed out of Chad, nonstop. Chad got excited when he found out that Shawn was not only in the ministry, but was reaching a generation that seems to have been forgotten by the local stained-glass churches. Don told me later that it was as if Chad was handing off the baton.

The next evening I went to visit Chad in his hospice room. When I arrived, the waiting area, which was like a huge living room, was full of young men. I was quickly told that Chad had begun to take a turn for the worse. Don and his son were keeping watch in Chad's room that night as the fight continued. I remember when I walked into Chad's room, his older brother Scott was sitting next to the bed. Scott was glued to Chad. You sensed that Scott was doing what he had done his entire life; picking up his little brother when he fell down. I was so encouraged watching that powerful scene of Scott caring for Chad when he was fighting during those final hours. I walked out of the room and began to visit with the guys that were hanging around the waiting area. The stories were amazing.

When Chad gave his life to the Lord, he gave it all away. Leaving a promising basketball career in California, he loaded up everything and drove to Texas. He first lived out of his car and then found an apartment. He shared and preached every chance he got. Not long after Chad arrived in Texas, he bought a huge tent and began nightly meetings where local down-and-out folks would wander in and hear about the love of God and how their lives were not meaningless and hopeless and that they mattered to Jesus.

His message was contagious.

Using basketball, Chad would go to the local gyms. He would purposely find the roughest part of town and the toughest group of kids. He would challenge them to games of one-on-one or just a pickup game. After gaining their attention and respect from basketball, he would share his message of hope with whoever would listen. The stories were incredible. One young man told a story of Chad walking into a gym on the east side of town. Chad was a young white kid, lean frame, and only six feet tall. He would purposely try to find the gyms that were full of black kids. That night he walked into a gym that was packed with local kids who were playing full-court games. When Chad walked in, everything came to a stop. Chad announced that he wanted to play the best player in the gym in a game of one-on-one. He said if he won he would get the floor for five minutes to share his faith with everyone there and he said if he lost they could "lynch me from the rafters." No one was lynched that night.

Chad converted to Christianity January 29. Chad's life verse became John 1:29—

"The next day John the Baptist saw Jesus coming toward him, and said,

"Behold! The Lamb of God who takes away the sin of the world!"

This verse became his life mission statement. Everywhere he went, people knew that Chad Matz's life message was John 1:29. It was his central theme. It defined him. It directed him.

The waiting room that night was full of young men who might have never heard the gospel unless Chad had risked rejection and humiliation. Person after person told stories of how, until they met Chad, they had no clue God cared or even knew who they were. One young man told me, "I didn't even know the story of Jesus was real until Chad sat me down and explained it in a way I understood."

I felt awkward that night. I had just met this family a few days before and did not want to intrude, but somehow I felt that I needed to be there. Not for Chad. He had an army of hurting, praying friends, but I felt I needed to be there for Don. I have a son. I could not imagine how he was able to make it through the day. I felt I needed to be there for Dad. Most of the kids in that waiting room could have been my own. I stayed for Don that night. I tried to pray for him as I watched him in the room sitting by his son's bed. What was going through his mind? Was it difficult to trust God? Did he feel abandoned by God? Would this event cause him to lean into God, or fall away?

The Butterfly Effect of Grace

Don told me when Chad knew his battle with cancer was nearing the end he had a tattoo of John 1:29, done on his stomach. The tattoo simply read,

John 1:29 "Behold! The Lamb of God who takes away the sin of the world!" He had it done in English and Greek.

Chad was determined that even when he was gone, the folks who would care for him after his death would be forced to see his life verse, John 1:29. It was his prayer that even that last person to have contact with his body would go home and maybe look up that verse, maybe for the first time read,

"The next day John saw Jesus coming toward him, and said, "Behold! The Lamb of God who takes away the sin of the world!"

The morning after I had been in the waiting room of the hospice center, I went back to see Don and to check on Chad. When I walked into the room, it was perfectly clean. The bed was made up and everything had been straightened. It is a cliché, but it felt like I was in a movie. Everyone was gone, including Chad. One of the day nurses walked in and I just blurted out, "Did Chad go home?" I know she knew what I meant, but she could not help it; she looked at me, smiled, and said, "Yes, he did, sir. Not to California, but he did go home." I instantly thought of Don. Before I could say anything, she told me his family was by his side and he went quietly during the night.

For a moment I didn't know what to do. My mind was racing trying to figure out what I should do next. I walked up to the nurses' station and thanked them for taking care

of Chad and for allowing the waiting area to accommodate
so many people the night before. As I walked away one
of the nurses said to me, "He did it, you know. We were
amazed that he literally willed himself to do it, but he did.
That was one determined kid!" I had no idea what she was
talking about, but she certainly thought I did. I asked. She
looked puzzled as if I was the only one that was not in on
the secret. She smiled and said,

"When Chad first arrived, he told us his goal was to hang
on until today. He made it to his goal."

She said, "Today is January 29. Chad wanted to make it
to January 29. He wanted his death certificate to read that
his date of death was January 29. His life verse was John
1:29. It says: 'Behold! The Lamb of God who takes away
the sin of the world!' He even had it tattooed on his belly.
Did you see it?"

I went and sat down in the waiting room. This time it was
empty and it was very quiet. I cried for Don. I cried for
Chad. I cried for his brother Scott. I cried for my son who
didn't die. I cried because a thirty-two-year-old kid, no wife,
no kids, who just wanted to help folks who are confused
and lost, died. He was gone. His voice was gone. His heart
was gone. His compassion was gone. It would have been
fine with me if God had healed his worn out body and he
had gone home, to California or Fort Worth, not heaven. It
just seemed too soon.

I cried for all of those reasons.

Chad's memorial service was held at a local funeral home
chapel. It was beyond standing room only. It was packed
with folks in the hall and against the side walls. It was

packed with folks Chad had done life with, so they were there for him now. There was not a coat and tie in the room. It was refreshing. It looked like we went to an inner-city park or playground and gathered up all the kids. It is hard to explain, but you could sense the room was packed with lots of people whose lives were literally rescued by one man who cared enough to share his story, one pickup game at a time.

Chad not only was good at basketball, but he also loved to write and read poetry. I'm not talking about "ring around the rosy" poems. I'm talking about Def Jam, hard-core, in-your-face poetry that is edgy and sometimes even harsh. But it gets to the heart of the matter. It is almost physical. You sense someone who is reading this kind of writing is about to explode with passion. Chad was a local favorite at poetry houses where people would get up and read their freelance writings.

At Chad's funeral, a single microphone was placed in the front of the chapel and a line instantly formed. One by one poets would get up and deliver the most powerful lines, almost in a sing-song fashion. It was fascinating. It seemed to lift the room. Almost all of the poems were about how Chad and his message had "saved their life." Not just from hell, but from a life *of* hell. Chad was able to help them connect the dots to God by caring for them and relating to them where they were. He didn't try and drag them into a church building; he dragged them to the foot of the cross and let Jesus do the changing. I remember thinking at one point during the service, "Where would these kids be right now if Chad had ignored the call of God on his life?"

At one point in the service one big guy on the back row shouted out,

"John chapter one, verse twenty nine: 'Behold! The Lamb of God who takes away the sin of the world!'"

It went completely silent for thirty seconds, not a word or a sound. I just smiled and I thought, "They got it. They got it. Mission accomplished, Chad, your message stuck!" I have never felt so at peace as I did sitting there in that room of folks who were so not "church folks" on the outside, but were so Jesus at heart. I got to watch fruit fall off the vine. Real fruit. Fruit that will matter and make a real difference. I kept thinking, "I don't know any of these people, but this is my family!"

I'm grateful I met Don that day in Kinko's. I remember I almost didn't say anything. I didn't want to appear nosy or rude. I'm glad I did. It changed my life. I would have missed all of this.

You would have too.

I like to imagine that right now some kid is about to walk inside a gym on the east side of town and challenge the best player to a game of one-on-one. Pray that he wins. Pray that everyone listens. Pray that everyone hears good news. Pray that at least one kid says,

"Why do you have John 1:29 tattooed on your arm?"

Pray that a butterfly effect of grace would cover that gym and that neighborhood.

We make a living by what we get,
but we make a life
by
what we give.
-Sir Winston Churchill

. . a widow who was poverty-stricken
came and put in two copper mites,
which together make half of a cent.
And He called His disciples and said to
them,
Truly I tell you, this widow, who is
poverty-stricken, has put in
more than all those contributing to the
treasury.
For they all threw in out of their
abundance; but she, out of her deep
poverty, has put in everything that she
had —
even all she had on which to live.
Mark 12:42-44 AMP

plastic pails and homemade pound cake.

I love pound cake. And I really love homemade pound cake. So, when she walked into my office offering a pound cake, I jumped up and ran over to the lobby where she was selling her cakes. She told me she was selling each one for ten dollars. I thought this was odd because she had never done this before. This was not a bag lady selling her goods door to door. This was a very classy lady in her sixties who I knew very well, and it just seemed odd that she was selling pound cakes in office buildings. Then she told me the reason she was doing this.

Her church was raising money.

This wasn't for new carpet. This wasn't for a new building just because the old building didn't fit the new style. This was money to help rebuild a church in Ecuador destroyed in an earthquake weeks earlier. Do you remember that one? Twenty-seven killed, hundreds injured, and thousands of homes leveled, leaving most of the villages in complete disarray. The economy was weak before the earthquake and now it was almost nonexistent. The damage was unimaginable. News pictures showed many cities in Ecuador were left in rubble.

That Sunday her pastor announced they would be sending a team of men into Ecuador to rebuild a church that had been destroyed. The material would have to be purchased when they got there; it could not be brought with them. The cost would be one hundred thousand dollars. The church did not have the extra money budgeted, but the pastor and his team felt called of God to go and help.

What did he do?
He gave everyone in the building two dollars.

Every person who walked out of the service took with
them two one dollar bills and a challenge to find a way
to multiply it. No instructions, no restrictions—only that it
be legal and ethical, and you needed to bring it back in
one week. So there she stood in my office with her pound
cakes. Don't you love it? This lady went straight to the
store, went home, and baked pound cakes.

When she told me the story, I asked her how many she
had with her; she told me she had three. I bought all three
and told her not to take the money back to church but to
take her thirty dollars and buy as many ingredients as she
could. I promised her I would buy any cakes she couldn't
sell from that batch. She didn't come back.

She sold them all.

She did that again and raised one hundred dollars all from
a two dollar seed.

This isn't about me being the pound cake mogul. It is about
a simple woman of God who was obedient to the charge
of her pastor and who went out and took a risk. She took a
risk of being laughed at, ignored, patronized, or completely
rejected. But she still stepped out and did what she could
do. She did what she had done for years and years: She
baked pound cakes. This time it mattered. Not that the
other times before didn't matter, but this time someone's
hope was on the line. A tiny village had been rocked to its
knees and this woman was simply obedient to God.

One of the best stories from that Sunday was a woman who was visiting the church while she was in town from Indiana to see her grandchildren. She sat quietly in the service that morning and listened as the pastor told the story of the village and the need they had. She was leaving to go back to Indiana that afternoon. What could she do?

She bought a plastic pail, the biggest one she could find for two dollars. That was the rule: Use it all but don't add to it. Trust God. *Trust* God. She did. She took the bucket to her office and told her co-workers the story of the village and the earthquake. She told them that her daughter's church was going to send a group to rebuild the little church. She told them it mattered to this village that the symbol of hope and faith be restored as they literally dug out of this disaster. She reminded them she had bought their kids' fundraiser stuff for years. When children and grandchildren of the employees brought around the little catalogue of overpriced items, all for a good cause, she always bought a little. This was payback. This time it wasn't cookie dough, candles, or bad cheesecake. It was people's lives—a place for these Ecuadorian people to find hope again.

Each floor passed the little pail from office to office and cubical to cubical until it got back to her. She emptied the little pail, added it up and went to her local bank and bought a money order. She went by the post office that afternoon and sent it back to her daughter's church for the trip to Ecuador. She hoped it would help.

She sent back a money order for $1,100.

The little pail cost two dollars. The risk of being laughed at, ignored, or rejected was also hers. For all she knew, those co-workers could have just stared her down and walked away. They could have tossed a few bills in and brushed her off. Somehow her message was straightforward, but genuine: Hey guys, this time it matters. Not that candles and peanuts don't matter for the local soccer team, but this time hope is waiting and we have a chance to ease some pain.

I read a story of a church in Atlanta whose pastor wanted to teach what it meant to give. When everyone walked into the worship center one Sunday, they were handed a sealed envelope and told not to open it until the end of the service. When the message was over everyone was told to open the envelope. To everyone's surprise there was a five dollar bill.

One single five dollar bill.

They were then told as they left the building that morning to pray and ask the Lord to lead them as to what to do with that five. They were told not just to give it to the first homeless person they ran into on the corner. Thought and prayer needed to be put into it. They also were told that, if they felt led to, they could add to it or go in with another person. The goal was simple: Make something special happen to someone with that five dollars. They were also told that they needed to do this during the next seven days and report back to the church how it went and how much they put toward the project.

By the next Sunday stories were everywhere. People found needs they never saw before. Lives were changed because folks were encouraged to step out, find the need, and make a difference. The part about adding to the five with your own money?

Three hundred thousand dollars.

Church members reported adding three hundred thousand dollars out of their own resources.

What's the point? What is the significance of the two dollars or the five dollars in the envelope? How did those few dollars cause folks to stretch and find out their hearts were bigger than they imagined?

What happened?

Those few dollars were a nest egg.

When you say "nest egg," most people think of a small savings account. Maybe a bank CD, or a little money tucked away in a jar or under the mattress. What could a nest egg possibly have to do with an earthquake in Ecuador or finding needs in inner-city Atlanta?

When farmers want to help their hens lay more eggs, or if a hen is not laying eggs at all, the farmer places an exact replica of an egg in the hen's nest. The egg is made out of wood and painted white, to look just like a real egg. When the hen sees that nest egg, she thinks she has laid the egg herself and somehow Mother Nature kicks in and the hen will either start laying eggs or lay even more than she has been laying. Though that nest egg wasn't hers, it encouraged and pushed her to produce what evidently was already inside.

The two dollars were just a nest egg.

The five dollar bill was just an encouragement, a seed to help birth what was already inside. Have you ever thought that maybe the money in your wallet or your purse is just a nest egg? Maybe God placed in your possession a seed to remind you that your money really is not yours. I am not suggesting that if you give away what you have, God is obligated to replace it and multiply it; He owes us nothing. Anything and everything He chooses to give is a blessing and an extension of His Grace. He can do what He wants, when He wants, without our permission or understanding. He is not a mean God; He is a good God. And there's a big difference. That being said, if I really do see all that I have as not my own but a gift from Him, then I should have no problem letting go of it,

Right?

What if we could see into the country of Ecuador right now? What if we could follow some of those people in that village to their church tonight as they sit there and live out their simple, genuine faith in a world that you and I may never ever relate to or comprehend? They deal with and live through heartache, sorrow, poverty, sickness, and disease that you and I most likely will never see. What if you could sit next to a family who lost a mom or a dad or both, or a set of young parents who lost their children in that earthquake? Do you think for a minute you would want back the ten dollars you gave up for a pound cake? See beyond the gift to the end. Find the butterfly effect in giving. The next time you stop to think whether or not you should open up and give to something, do it.

Don't analyze it.
Just give.
Always be a giver.

Always.

In Vegas, I got into a long argument with
the man at the roulette wheel over what
I considered to be an odd number.
-Steven Wright

Come, let us sing for joy
to
the
LORD;
let us shout aloud to the
Rock
of our salvation.
Psalm 95:1 NIV

jesus and las vegas.

I did it. I included the words Las Vegas in this book and the earth did not split. I may have just lost some of you that think only sin and bad people live in Las Vegas. Sin and bad people are in your town too, and there are also wonderful people in Las Vegas. We'll get to that later. For some of you, I would have lost you at hello if I had opened the book with this chapter. But stay with me; it gets good.

My son plays guitar. He plays acoustic, electric, and with gritted teeth, classical. He even plays the mandolin. He is good. He plays in a worship band at our church, he plays camps, retreats, etc., and he loves great Christian bands. One of his favorite, and mine, is the David Crowder Band. If you know the Crowder band, then you know they are incredible. In my opinion David Crowder is a modern day prophet. God seems to speak so clearly and powerfully through his music. I love his music. The words God gives him are amazing. Read the words to his songs; don't just listen to them, but read them. It will help you connect the dots to God.

If you've raised kids, especially if they're twenty-something, you know that odd feeling of looking at your kids and wondering, "Did I give them enough to make it? Did I pray for them enough? I trust God, but I don't trust my ability to be a great parent. Will my children follow after God long after I am gone and out of their lives? Are they really in love with Jesus, or is this just a phase they will grow out of?" I know that really sounds like doubt and fear, and some of it is, but if you have raised kids past their teen years into young adulthood, then you know that feeling. You've poured the concrete, it's dry, and you are about to pull the forms away and see if it's level or crooked. Raise up a child in the admonition of the Lord and when they are old they will not depart from their ways. I read that. I need to trust that.

Back to Crowder. I was looking at their schedule on the internet and discovered they were opening for Third Day, another great band. I looked across and saw that they were playing at the House of Blues in Las Vegas. That just sounds cool, right? House of Blues, Mandalay Bay, Las Vegas. So we went. Viva Las Vegas. We loaded up and went with two other couples and our boys.

We made our way into the House of Blues on a Friday night to see the Crowder Band and Third Day. The place was packed. Jam packed. I know it was way past fire marshal capacity. As the time approached for the first band to come out, it got really tight down on the floor where we were. By the time they came out, I could have lifted my feet off the ground and I might not have fallen. It was tight. So when the Crowder Band came out the place went nuts.

One of my favorite memories happened that night. My son, my buddy Scott, and I were down on the floor just a few feet in front of the stage; it was loud! Our wives would wave to us occasionally as they stood back where the uncommitted and non-hearing-impaired were safe from the blast of the speakers. Wimps. Here I was forty-four years old jamming with the teens and twenty-somethings trying hard not to embarrass my son.

At one point they started this jumping thing, where everyone just jumps as high as they can. That's it; just jump like you are on fire, straight up as high as you can. Just jump. Keep jumping. Not left or right, just straight up in the air. It was so cool for the first fifteen seconds. The only problem was that it becomes the most amazing aerobic exercise you can imagine after the fifteen seconds is long gone. We kept jumping, straight in the air. Suddenly I got that feeling you get when you are over forty and not exactly in Olympic shape. It is the feeling of "O my gosh, is this a heart attack? Or am I just going to die from lack of breath?"

They kept jumping and I began to imagine my son standing over me as the paramedics did CPR. I just pictured him thinking, "Wow, I am SO embarrassed. The concert has come to a screeching halt because my nine-hundred-year-old, out of shape dad died from jumping in place." I also tried to imagine what an idiot I would look like if I just stopped jumping and stood there and watched while everyone else kept jumping. Same "o my gosh" picture of my son as he looked back over his shoulder at me sweating like a goat, panting out of breath like I just finished the New York marathon.

So, I just kept jumping, and finally everyone stopped. I was very glad the maniacal jumping had ceased. I owe the Lord two weeks of missionary work in the worst corner of the world as a swap for that miracle.

Beyond almost dying in Las Vegas from jumping up and down at the HOB, I discovered something wonderful. I began to ask people where they were from. There were lots of high school and college age students. Lots of adults were there with those students so I asked them where they were from. These were neat groups of kids. They just looked like they were having a blast. It was worship to a God that they seemed to have really connected with. It was contagious to be around them and to see their joy at celebrating who God was in their lives. Students focused on the heart of God. It was great. When people started telling me where they were from I was stunned. Almost everyone that was on the floor, lots of students and adults, were from the same town.

Las Vegas.

Pop quiz: Where would you have thought they were from? When you think of God-fearing, Christ-following, Jesus people, do you think of the little village of Las Vegas? No, you don't. Why? Truth is, we all are just religious enough not to want to think that the love of God flows through towns like Vegas. Truth is, why wouldn't the love of God flow right through the middle of that town and every other place in the world that needs the love of Christ? Other than the neon lights and odds makers, is there really any difference between Las Vegas and the town you grew up in? Ok, besides that. It's in your town too, just not as famous!

Almost every major industry in the world hosts its annual convention in Las Vegas. Some people who normally would never ever dream of stepping foot in Las Vegas go there every year or so for a convention or trade show. It is the fastest growing city in the United States. There are some of the best churches in and around Las Vegas. I guarantee that UNLV, which is a major university there, has a Campus Crusade for Christ, BSU, or some other evangelical organization that is trying desperately to connect with college students.

Someone is praying for those students right now, tonight, in Las Vegas.

At least one person is on their knees right now in Las Vegas, Nevada, somewhere, praying for someone in that town.

When I was standing in the HOB at Mandalay Bay in Las Vegas, watching people sing at the top of their lungs, I thought, "Jesus said, where two or more of you are gathered in my name there I will be also." I looked around and started laughing, "Jesus is here somewhere." I take that verse literally. I really do believe that, for some reason, when He said it He meant it, literally. Jesus was walking through that place watching His kids have a blast worshiping Him. Maybe He was keeping me from falling over dead from jumping. Who knows? He knows. That night Jesus was in Las Vegas. He's there tonight. He lives there because at least two of His children meet in His name daily, somewhere in that town.

Wow.

I also got to experience something that night I will never forget. It was as if I got to see my son be born all over again, spiritually. I was standing just behind him during the entire concert and at one point when Crowder was singing "Here is our King," my son lifted one hand in the air, and was singing at the top of his lungs. It stopped me. I instantly flashed back to when he was a tiny little boy in first grade or maybe even kindergarten. How many times did he raise his hand in class when he knew the answer? How many times during P.E. did he raise his hand to say, "Pick me. I want to be on the team!" I just could not keep from thinking, "Thank God, he knows the answer! Pick him, Lord."

He gets it.

His generation gets it.

My son understands that the Kingdom of God is much more than a choir robe and offering plate. He has already been infected with the truth that goes way beyond board meetings and buildings. My son and his generation will never settle for the status quo. He will never be religious *for religion's sake*. He'll never sit on the back row in a suit and tie on Sunday morning sleeping through a boring sermon, because that's just what you do. He will sit in a coffee house with torn blue jeans and have a heart for God that you and I may never see.

Of all the things that will claw and fight for the attention and affection of his tender heart, my prayer is that his generation will do it better than mine did. God is worthy of his twenty-year-old heart. When I saw him that night I just started crying, not a lot, still in the no-embarrassment zone, but I just could not hold it back. My baby was growing up in the Lord, and it was awesome to have a front row seat to watch it that night. He could have been at any show that night. He was at this one and it was good. It was very good. If you know David Crowder, tell him thank you for teaching a generation of kids and adults that God is right here. Tell him thank you for leading my son to the throne room of God, even with a ring tone on his cell phone. Yep, don't underestimate the tiny ways that God uses the simple things in life. First time I heard my son's cell phone ring with one of Crowder's songs busting out, I just had to laugh. I laughed at the fact that even though you and I may get stuck in our religious ruts, God seems to keep moving through one generation to the next.

It is wild to think that before the world was spoken into existence, God saw fit to fill up the House of Blues, in Las

Vegas, Nevada, with kids who love Him. They danced; they sang; they jumped in the air until I almost died. They worshiped God that night. I did too. When the concert was done, they left the House of Blues, and I am certain that the kingdom of God grew in depth and someone met Christ in a new, fresh way. It was raw, it was real, and it renewed my hope that the next generation is just fine with their tattoos and piercings and spiked hair; they will carry an old message of hope in a new wineskin.

You can bet on it.

Few people are interested in a religion
that has nothing to say to the world
and offers them only life after death,
when what people are really wondering
is whether there is life before death.
The Irresistible Revolution:
Living as an Ordinary Radical

Let no one despise or think less of
you because of your youth, but be an
example or pattern for the believers in
speech, in conduct,
in love,
in faith,
and in purity.
1 Tim 4:12 AMP

rain clouds and port-o-lets.

I know adding a chapter about Louie Giglio and the Passion conferences is like cheating off of Alan Greenspan in a college economics class. If you don't know who Alan Greenspan is, that reference will make no sense. Google it. Anything Louie and Passion do is so amazing, in my humble opinion, that adding it here feels a little odd. Case in point. I bought a book about Rick Warren, the lead teaching pastor at Saddleback Church in California. I bought the book, thinking it would be an interesting read about Rick Warren and the history of Saddleback. It was a rewrite of his book *The Purpose Driven Life*. It felt more like a wikipedia chapter on Rick Warren. I felt a bit cheated. I don't want to be guilty of that in this chapter.

My history with this ministry dates back to the late '80s into the early '90s. I was a worn out youth pastor running around the country speaking to camps and weekend groups of kids, serving at a church that was going through a tough transition. I was tired. Louie did a weekly Monday night service at a church right on the Baylor campus. The service was called Choice and the format was simple: strong worship, solid teaching, every Monday night. I knew if I could find my way into Seventh & James Street Baptist Church by seven o'clock I would be able to make it through the next week. Right or wrong, it kept me going, and many nights it seemed God exposed His heart in a new way. Those nights at Choice are a part of who I am today. I would be different without that experience.

So, years later when someone was rounding up a group to go to work in Memphis at OneDay, I said yes. OneDay was an event that lasted three days. I know; you can't call it

OneDay and have it last over three days, but they did. The plan was this: Tell an entire generation of college students there is an event in Memphis, Tennessee, where great worship and strong teaching is all outdoors. Bring your own tents, blankets, food, and water. It wasn't free; you pay thirty dollars to get in the gate. No transportation provided; get there on your own. It would be out on a four thousand acre farm with no modern conveniences, like wireless internet, cable or TV. Keep in mind this was the twenty-something group. Think anyone showed up?

Thirty thousand.

They flew, they drove, they hitchhiked, they rode buses, they figured out how to get there.

When we arrived, most of the structure was already set up. It was an ocean of people everywhere. The funniest scene was the long line of port-o-lets on one side of the field, set one against the other. It was quite a Kodak moment. Huge stage, enormous video screens, monster speakers; you get the picture. It looked at times like those shots you see in Central Park in New York City at an open air concert with people packed in by the thousands. It had that feel. But this was different. This was a generation in the late '90s that had discovered a very basic, yet profound truth; this was not their father's religion. This group didn't need Wednesday night supper and committee meetings. They didn't wear suits and ties. They couldn't care less if the church bus got a tune up, but it did bother them a lot that injustice seemed to rule the world. They were passionate about what they believed and they were not ashamed to express it. They lived their faith out loud and could not give a hoot if you thought they were irreverent about it. When they knew the answer, they raised their hand. It seemed they knew the answer a lot those three days.

The secret of Passion is really no secret at all. Love God, love people. Take that message across the street and around the world. Everyone is a missionary, regardless of where you work or where you live. If you have the love of Christ in your heart, it was put there to be given away. Don't complicate the gospel with rules. To me the most refreshing thing about Passion is that it appears to have no structure at all. I don't mean it is disorganized. Pulling off the kinds of events they do demands tremendous planning and vision. I just mean it doesn't look like every other organization in the evangelical world. I am certain that they have the charter, books, and budgets to keep the government and board members happy. But it feels like, above everything else, Christ is lifted up. He is the focus of the teaching, the music, the worship; He is the main thing. How odd—Christ being the main thing of a Christian movement?

The schedule of this three day, OneDay event was a balance of music, teaching, and prayer. Some of the speakers were Beth Moore, John Piper, Voddie Baucham, and Louie. The worship was led by Chris Tomlin, David Crowder, Charlie Hall, Matt Redman, and others. Even though it was all about Jesus, these were no lightweights to sit under. It was powerful. They got up in front of the students and adults and challenged them to love God and to express that love to a world desperately in need of truth. It was simple, but life changing.

At one point in the afternoon, as I was watching thousands of college students genuinely love God out loud, I thought, "This generation is ruined." In a good way. No more systems. No more agendas. This generation will charge hell with a water pistol. I kept thinking how refreshing it was to see these kids with hearts and hands lifted up to God for all the right reasons. This wasn't Thursday night at camp. This wasn't a local denominational conference, voting on the next super hero. This was a group, a very large group, of students being challenged to run to the corners of the earth and love people into eternity. No pamphlets, no bumper stickers. Just tell the world they are loved unconditionally by the God of the universe and He will forgive and restore them from the inside out. Tell them the gospel is good news. It is not a big hairdo and multi-million dollar buildings. It stands on its own. It is not another goofy TV preacher. No defense needed. Tell people you love them because God placed that in your heart. Stand there until they get it or they reject it. But go, and stand.

In one afternoon session, Louie asked if anyone had sensed God was leading them to go to a foreign mission field—to go to a country that they may not be able to find on a map, and where they may not speak the language or understand the culture. He asked them to stand to their feet. Hundreds of students stood up. Some looked bold and excited; some looked like they were about to ride a roller coaster for the first time. But they stood to their feet. Louie asked us to gather around those students, lay our hands on them, and pray for them. He then said,

"I want you to go to a foreign land and never come home."

It was a heavy moment. I don't know how many of those students are somewhere tonight, doing what they felt they were called to do, living out their life in a new land. I do know that every one of them that did do that brought glory to God.

I have been to other Passion events. They all seem to present the same, consistent theme: The glory of God is supreme. The speakers, the music, the worship, the entire event all points to the heart and soul of God, which is His glory. Simple, but easily missed.

I believe God is doing a new, different, and final work. Final in that it is preparing the way for Christ to return. I have no idea when that will be. I do know this: He is coming back to get us. He is coming back to set everything right. He is going to clean the slate and write a new song, new word, and make a new beginning. It is all going to close some day, and reopen under new management. Everything will stop and everything will start over. New kingdom, new King, new future. And I believe that He is beginning that new work in the hearts of the kids that have been and are now coming out of our high schools and colleges. That age group. That tender heart. I do know that there is massive confusion and disbelief in that group. I know we are seeing students make very bad choices that are resulting in scarred lives. The statistics are mind-bending. An entire generation is being misled by a university system that, in large part, sends them down a dangerous path.

I get that.

However, I really do believe God is building a remnant. I believe He is speaking a new word of hope and encouragement and faith to the hearts and minds of our students. I have so much hope for this group that are fast becoming our next generation of adults. I see a group of students who have a reckless abandon to running after the things of God. They almost don't care, in a good way. They seem not to be waiting on you and me to catch up with their fire and faith. As I have said many times in this book, they are not going to "do church" like you and I did. They are busy "being" the church, while you and I are laying bricks and mortar, thinking we are building the kingdom of God. All to honor a God that says He dwells not in temples made by human hands (Acts 7:48, 17:24). It is something I just cannot get out of my heart.

I had one of those moments a few months back. I was headed out to meet a client in the front lobby of our office. The ladies in the front reception room could see me and they could see the gentleman in the lobby waiting on me, but they knew I could not see him yet. They were giggling knowing I was not prepared for what I was about to see. When I got to the lobby, I introduced myself to a man who was about my age, maybe a few years older. Blue jeans, leather vest, do-rag on his head, earrings, tattoos, gold and silver necklaces. We walked into my office and began to discuss why he was there. I noticed he was wearing one of those rubber "Lance Armstrong"-type bracelets, but it had the letters jctv.org; I just could not resist. I asked him what that stood for. He frantically looked around my office to find some assurance that he was not about to jump off a bridge with his answer. He looks at me and says,

"Dude, I know I don't look like it, but I'm a born again Christian, for real!"

We both laughed at his answer. I knew what he meant. I asked him what the jctv.org was for and he told me. Some Christian television deal he was pumped about. I let him go on for a bit and then I asked him how he found the Lord. He looked at me and then blurted out,

"I'm a recovern' drug addict and a recovern' Southern Baptist."

I told him I was too. He asked me what drug I was hooked on and I explained that I meant the second part. We both laughed. He told me that a buddy had asked him to go to an outdoor rock-n-roll concert at the Texas Motor Speedway one Saturday night. Off they went. Twenty minutes into the concert he asked his buddy why no one was drinking beer. His buddy told him these were Christian rock bands. He didn't like that, but he stayed. Somehow during the concert, the dots to God were connected. He gave his life to the Lord. He was so excited that he went back home to his mom's church. He said it didn't take long before he figured out they were not happy that his newfound faith came with tattoos, earrings, and a past. He was not welcomed in the one place he should have been welcomed with open arms. So, as he put it, he now goes to a church "for people like me." They get together and sing, listen to teaching, fellowship, feed the hungry, visit the prisoners and their families, make sure those without housing find a place to stay. He looked at me with absolutely no arrogance and said,

"We do the things you guys just talk about."

Ouch.

Does he do the things your church just talks about?

I was talking to a new teacher in our town the other day. I asked her where she was from; she told me Waco. We small talked a bit about both of us going to Baylor and who we knew in Waco. Somehow the subject of Louie Giglio and the Choice Bible study came up. Her mother worked at Baylor and in the mid '80s told her daughter that an intern who worked in her office was starting a Bible study. She told her daughter this young man was wonderful and that she should go to this Bible study. She did. It was one of the first Bible studies Louie held.

That afternoon I got an e-mail with an attachment and a note that said, "Found this picture my mom sent me in the mid '80s when she worked at Baylor. Thought you would enjoy it!" I opened the attachment and it was a picture of this lady's mom, with her arm around this kid. Big bushy hair, big glasses, skinny as a rail, huge grin on his face. It was Louie, and he looked fifteen years old. I know he was in his '20s, obviously, but he looked so young and so innocent. Just looked like any kid on any college campus. Just posing for a picture with some random teacher. That's all. That's all?

When I looked at the picture, before any of Passion or the Choice meetings had taken place, I thought of what it must have been like for God to be building this vision in Louie's heart. What was that like? When was the first time he began to dream, even on the smallest scale? Remember, God calls the end from the beginning; never an accident. Before Louie was born, God saw fit to begin the process of bringing all of this together for His glory.

One afternoon at the OneDay event in Memphis a horrible rain storm came up. It had been misting, sprinkling, and raining off and on, but this was different. Way back behind us this huge, black and almost green cloud was approaching. For those of us who grew up in tornado alley, we knew what that cloud looked like. It was trouble. You could sense the uneasiness in the masses. All I could imagine was how bad it was about to get. Hail stones would pound this group of students. The video screens and speaker towers would come crashing down. This was going to get ugly fast.

Then, as if it was a movie set and this was all computer generated, that black cloud broke in half and moved around us. It moved around us. As it passed by on either side you felt and heard a hushed awe. Faith rose up in that crowd—not in what they could do, but in what God had just done. It was perfect. What a setup for God to demonstrate that even the atmosphere is in the palm of His hand.

I am sure the local weather man could explain what happened in very technical terms, but you will never wipe that visual from the minds of those college students. They were there. They knew what was about to happen. Then God said, "Peace be still." The clouds obeyed. The crisis was averted. God's glory was magnified. All in five minutes. OneDay was a good day. Even though it was three days.

Character cannot be developed in ease
and quiet.
Only through experience of
trial and suffering
can the soul be strengthened,
ambition inspired,
and success achieved.
Helen Keller 1880 - 1968

The LORD does not look at the things
man looks at.
Man looks at the outward appearance,
but the LORD
looks at the heart.
1 Sam 16:7 NIV

karen.

It seems like yesterday I sat in a board room surrounded by men staring at me. There were questions on my ministry philosophy and how I would "do better" than the last guy. Somehow I made it through those confirmation hearings and was offered the student minister position. For the past three years I had traveled and spoken to students, and I was looking forward to being with them up close and personal, which I knew would be very different and very challenging.

I was right.

It was the first week, if not the first day, when someone said to me, "Have you met Karen?" It wasn't the last time I heard that question. The pastor wanted me to make sure I met Karen. The first time I visited with my secretary, she asked if I had met Karen. I had been in student ministry long enough that many thoughts went through my mind. Do I want to meet Karen? Are they warning me, or trying to prepare me for a junior high student from, well, you get the idea? Needless to say, I was a bit concerned about my first encounter with Karen.

Then I did meet Karen.
And it changed my life.

Let me introduce you to Karen. This is Karen's story, in her own words. With her and her mother's permission I share this with you.

I was born in April of 1975 with a condition known as Goldenhar's Syndrome. It affects people in different

78

ways but it causes craniofacial deformities. In my case, I
was born without a right ear, lung, or thumb. In addition,
I am missing some of the bones on the right side of my
face including my right jawbone. This gives my face an
asymmetrical appearance. I was born with a cleft lip
and palate which were repaired when I was very young.
Although this wasn't discovered until a few years ago, I
was also born with an atrial septal defect (hole between
the top two chambers of my heart). Finally, I began to
develop scoliosis (curvature of the spine) at about the age
of five. This became and is still considered to be a severe
curvature. I can't stand up completely straight or hold
my head straight and there is a hump on my back. As far
as surgeries go, I have had a total of seven operations.
Most people with this syndrome have many more but
my parents and I together with the physicians involved
in my care made the decision not to pursue extensive
reconstruction on my face. Because I only have one lung
and also because it is extremely difficult to intubate me
(put a tube down my throat during surgery to enable the
anesthesiologist to maintain an airway during surgery),
it was decided that the risks outweighed the potential
benefits of reconstructive surgery in my particular situation.
I should also mention that I have a growth hormone
deficiency so even though I am now 32 years old, I am still
only 4 feet 7 inches tall and weigh 75 pounds.

Karen attended a high school with over 2,500 students.
She would sometimes slip out of class a few minutes early
so she could get to the next class before the mob of other
kids would have surely trampled her. Karen lives in Dallas,
Texas, where it seems that everyone is cosmetically and
surgically perfect, no matter what the cost or pain. Every
ad on TV screams to our need, our desperate need, to look
beautiful and appear healthy 24/7; even if we are not.

Karen understands and loves God more than we ever will.

Karen takes nothing for granted.
Nothing.
You and I do every day.
Every minute of every day.

Yes we do.

Karen's mother, Pat, tells a powerful story of when she was first approached by the doctor that delivered Karen. He began to tell her the different problems that Karen was born with. She said all she could think was, "Stop telling me these things!" The list kept going. Pat said she was headed to a Bible study one morning as she was dealing with this overwhelming challenge of caring for this new born with so many medical and life challenges. She said she walked into the room and even though the teacher had no idea what she was going through she had written on the board this verse;

Isaiah 55:8 'My thoughts are not your thoughts, and neither are your ways my ways, declare the Lord'.

Can you imagine that morning how that sentence must have leaped off the board? Pat told me the passage of scripture that carried her through many difficult days and nights was Psalm 139:13-16.

"For you created my inmost being; you knit me together in my mother's womb. I praise you because I am fearfully and wonderfully made; your works are wonderful, I know that full well. My frame was not hidden from you when I was made in the secret place. When I was woven together in the depths of the earth, your eyes saw my unformed body.

All the days ordained for me were written in your book before one of them came to be."

Read that again, and this time try and picture what it was like when Pat watched Karen fall asleep at night. There had to be more than one night when she stood on the edge of her faith, leaning over into doubt, wondering how this could bring Glory to God. It did. How many nights did her faith whisper to Karen, "God is great, and He is very, very good. You can trust Him. He makes no mistakes. You are a perfectly formed gift from Heaven."

I remember the first time I sat down with Karen for a one-on-one conversation. She told me her favorite passage of scripture was where Samuel is sent by God to anoint the new king of Israel. He goes to the house of Jesse, in Bethlehem, who has eight sons. One of the first sons brought before Samuel is Eliab, David's older brother. According to the text, Eliab is a strong, handsome warrior who Samuel thinks is the new King of Israel. But look at what happens:

"When they arrived, Samuel saw Eliab and thought, 'Surely the Lord's anointed stands here before the LORD.' But the LORD said to Samuel, 'Do not consider his appearance or his height, for *I have rejected him*. The LORD does not look at the things man looks at. *Man looks at the outward appearance*, but the LORD looks at the heart.'" I Samuel 16:6-7

Karen said, "Knowing that the Lord looks at my heart gives me comfort."

One year we went to a large camp with 1,500 students from all over the state. On a Tuesday night Karen got up and told her life story. She told how God was her source of strength. She said that even though she had many opportunities to question God for how she was born, she never did because she knew and understood that God never makes mistakes. She said she knew she was not an accident or just an incident; she was created by God, for God. She told about how when she felt afraid before a surgery or alone in a large crowd of people she remembered the unconditional love and acceptance of God. As she talked, Karen seemed to have a connection with God that was different and real. The thorn in her side, that would never go away, seemed to bring an intimacy and fellowship that amazed me.

She read her story from a piece of paper, never looking up at the crowd, and then quietly sat down. There was silence. You knew everyone there just heard the truth. You knew this was a moment you would never forget. We didn't. After that brief silence, the entire place gave her a standing ovation. Karen always got a standing ovation. You could not remain seated after you heard her story.

It was as if in five minutes Karen helped every person in that place understand, for the first time, *you have no problems*.

You have much to be grateful for.
Life is precious.
Life is a gift.
God is good.

You and I are so self absorbed.
Yes, we are.

Karen didn't say that or even try to suggest it, but the message of her story said it very clearly.

Oh, by the way, Karen would tell you that *she* has no problems either. When Karen emailed her story to me, the title of the email was, "Romans 8:28, and we know that all things work together for good, to those that love God and who are called according to His purpose." Even for her, every day is a gift from God, to be lived with hope and joy. And someone, somewhere is always going through something much worse than you are right now. Wow. Perspective?

The speaker for the camp that week was a man named Dave Busby. If you ever heard Dave speak you know he was a very powerful speaker. Not much rocked Dave's world. He had his own valley of pain to walk through, having been born with cystic fibrosis and developed polio at a very early age. He lived and walked in a depth with God that staggered everyone's imagination. Dave was scheduled to get up and speak after Karen's testimony that night. He was sitting just a few chairs down from me and I remember he just sat there and stared at the stage. Karen had already sat down, to a standing ovation. When Dave got up to speak he seemed baffled and distracted. He asked his wife to come up on stage and pray for him before he spoke. She did and he delivered a powerful message.

Later that week at breakfast Dave told me that Karen's story disturbed him so much that he completely lost his train of thought. He told me that her humility and transparency were so thick on the stage when he got up he felt he needed to take off his shoes and run out the back. He told me that the cloud was heavy on stage when he got up to speak and that Karen had rearranged the platform. After hearing Karen speak the heart of God that night, he wasn't sure why he even tried to follow her.

I told him he should try and be her youth pastor. He said no thank you, last night was hard enough.

One student minister told me his group of students went back to their cabin and talked for hours about what Karen said. It set the tone for the week and even the summer for those students. They saw a living, breathing example of what it means to live life to the fullest, no matter what.

I remember one night Karen got up in front of the youth group and asked them to forgive her for not being a bolder witness at her high school campus. One of her friends looked up at me and just shook her head as if to say, "She is the most powerful witness on that campus just by the way she lives her life. How can she think she has let us or God down?" The bar had just been set much higher.

My favorite memory of Karen was her high school graduation. Her graduating class was enormous, 639 students. Karen was almost at the end of the list alphabetically, so by the time she walked the stage we all were pretty worn out. When the school official called out her name and she walked across the stage, her class began to clap. Then they stood up and gave Karen a standing ovation. The coolest sight was when one of the first people to stand up was Greg Ostertag, one of her class mates. Greg is the seven-foot basketball center who later played for the Utah Jazz. Greg began the standing ovation that night as if to say, "Karen, I've always looked *up* to you!"

I could tell you story after story of Karen—about how many times other students told me she made them think differently about their own lives and how they were challenged to live a life that was worthy of imitation. I remember driving home at night after a youth event that Karen was at and wondering what she would be doing years later—how *her* life would continue to *bring* life to others.

The thing I learned most from Karen was how simple it is to lead others to a deeper walk just by living a quiet, genuine life. It doesn't have to be famous, or fast, or strong, or bold. It just has to be real.

Karen's faith had a color and a sound. It was bright and it was loud. If you knew Karen you would know this to be an odd description of her. Karen does not draw attention to herself. Karen is not loud. She is quiet and soft spoken. But I believe if faith gives off a color in heaven, Karen's faith is like a rainbow that has no end and no beginning. And if faith has a sound, Karen's must sound like a 1,000 voice choir. So the next time you need a visual of what faith may look like to those of us who need to be reminded every day that what we do, how we respond and react to the hand that is dealt to us here on earth, ask yourself this question. What shade of faith does the world need to see in my life, and is my faith a whisper or a shout?"

Karen also taught me that life is sometimes difficult. Life is sometimes painful. It is sometimes confusing and harsh and unfair. But life is also a gift from God. It is a package to be opened every day. Don't look at what you don't have, but be thankful for what you do have; your life is His design.

It is His plan.
It is His purpose.
He has never second guessed a decision.
He built Karen from scratch; it was a good day.
It was a very good day.

If you've never met Karen, you've missed one of the most incredible people in the world. Karen reminds me daily of the simplicity of the good news of the gospel. If ever there was an icon for the butterfly effect of grace, it is Karen. Everyone who has come in contact with her will tell you today that she changed their life. Even today I will run into student ministry colleagues that met Karen and they will always ask about her.

Thank you, Karen, for allowing me to share your incredible life story. I know you are never one to seek out the spotlight. You need to know you changed my life. And now with your permission I have extended that reach.

Unfortunately I cannot remember all the students' names I worked with over the years.

I will never forget Karen Yates.

Karen, God used you to open my eyes to so much. I remember sentences you said to me. I remember where I was standing when you told me your favorite passage of scripture and why it was so special to you. I remember the look on your face when we had that awesome graduation party for you. I remember when you sat down after speaking at different events, almost baffled at why everyone was still clapping and still standing.

Karen, I have never told you this before, but every time I read the last chapter of Max Lucado's book *The Applause of Heaven*, I think of you. Max ends that book with a picture of what it might be like when we enter heaven for the first time:

"You'll be home soon too. You may not have noticed it, but you are closer to home than ever before. Each moment is a step taken. Each breath is a page turned. Each day is a mile marked, a mountain climbed. You are closer to home than you've ever been. Before you know it, your appointed arrival time will come; you'll descend the ramp and enter the City. You'll see faces that are waiting for you. You'll hear your name spoken by those who love you. And, maybe, just maybe—in the back, behind the crowds—the One who would rather die than live without you will remove his pierced hands from his heavenly robe and....applaud."

Karen, it won't be your first standing ovation.
But this one will last for what seems like an eternity.

"I doubt whether the world holds for any one,
a more soul-stirring surprise
than the first adventure
with
ice cream."
-Heywood C. Broun 1888-1939

He will wipe away all tears from their eyes, and there shall be no more death, nor sorrow, nor crying, nor pain. All of that has gone forever.
Rev 21:4 TLB

ice cream.

A few years ago I lost a good friend to cancer. It was hard to watch him fight the disease, but he was brave. I remember one afternoon when he finished chemo treatments; he felt terrible, but he came to the house anyway just to sit and watch movies. He got sick a few times but seemed to enjoy the diversion of the movie. He never complained. He loved to laugh. I can still hear that goofy laugh of his. We had a birthday party for him at our house. It would be the last birthday party before he died. In our living room we still have pictures framed from that party.

I didn't want him to die. I had only met him one year before he died when I heard about his diagnosis and went by to see how he was and if there was anything we could do. I would have loved to see him come through and beat that cancer. When he was diagnosed with brain cancer, the doctors gave him a very slim chance to survive. I prayed they were wrong. In fact, I remember getting up one morning and noticing my hand was sore. I could not figure it out. Then I remembered banging my fist on the steering wheel the day before begging God to let him live. I would beg God every day to take the cancer away. I didn't care where He sent it, just as long as He took it away from my friend. That's the honest truth. I kept explaining to God that He would receive glory by healing my friend. I kept trying to convince God that it would be a great testimony of how wonderful His power was if he beat the cancer and lived to tell the story.

My friend was dying.
My friend was losing his battle to brain cancer.

The treatments were so hard and made him so sick.
My friend was so full of life.
My friend just wanted to feel better.
My friend was tired of hospitals and doctors.

My friend was four years old.

Only four years old.

Four.

Somehow that changes the story, doesn't it?

When I would ask him how old he was, he would carefully tuck his thumb under and hold up four tiny little fingers and stick them high in the air and scream out, "Four!" He only had four birthday parties. Holding up those four fingers were not enough. I prayed for at least five fingers. He died with ten fingers and ten toes. That would have been twenty digits to hold up. Twenty would have been so much better than four.

I have known people who battled cancer. Some of them have died. Some survived. I have watched those amazing kids and the wonderful staff at St. Jude Children's Research Hospital and the incredible work they do to battle childhood cancer. My wife and I have sent them money in support of what they do. But for us, this was very different. This little boy was in our home. He called me by my name. He ate at my kitchen table. He napped on my sofa when he just plain ran out of gas. We prayed for him by name. We drove to the hospital late at night when he would get so sick from the cancer and the treatment. For almost a year, it seemed to be the only thing we did. It was the hardest year of our life and he wasn't even our child. We only had to watch from the sidelines. I can't imagine the pain down on the field each day. As hard as we tried to help, we always went home each night to our son, who was home, without cancer. Sometimes it was hard to know what to say.

One day he and his mother were sitting in the garden area at the hospital where he was getting treatments. He was playing in the grass when a man from a local church walked up. It was obvious that our little friend was very sick. His head was bald, with a large "zipper" incision cut from one side to the other. He was pale white and the medicine caused him to swell up. He looked like a little boy with cancer. This man looked at the mother and son and then said to the mother,

"You know, if you just have enough faith Jesus will heal your son."

Let that scene soak in.

I'm sure this man, in some twisted way, thought he was doing some good, somehow stating what everyone else had missed.

She looked back at this man and said,

"I carried this baby inside of me for nine months, I nursed this child, and I have raised this little boy the past four years every day of his life. Do you really think there is one single human being in the world that wants to see him healed of cancer more than me, his mother? I beg God every day to spare his life. You have no idea how much faith is inside me right now just to keep going every day."

Good answer.

When will we learn that God is not sitting in heaven wringing His hands, nervous that one of us is going to place a checker on the wrong square and mess up His entire game? I believe in prayer. I told you I prayed every day that God would heal my friend of cancer. He didn't. He didn't heal my friend, a four-year-old child, of cancer. He could have, couldn't he? Was it out of His reach? Didn't He promise that He would hear our prayers? Jesus Himself healed people in the New Testament. He raised people from the dead. Why did He choose to allow my little buddy to die? Wouldn't it have been okay if this chapter was about how he fought through the treatments and surgeries and survived? It could have been about how people banded together and prayed and fasted and finally one day he was announced cancer free. Today he would be twelve years old. I would be just fine with that. I would have eight more birthday pictures in my family room. But I only have one.

Why?

Why did God allow him to die?

If you don't answer that question, you may cave in on every other question. Why would God allow something that painful, if He didn't have a deeper purpose? What if somehow everything that happens is part of a master plan to bring glory to God, especially in the most difficult of circumstances?

Even the death of a four-year-old child?

I remember sitting in a service one night at Willow Creek Community Church in Chicago and the pastor, Bill Hybels, told an amazing story. He said he was getting ready to speak to a group of parents at their church. This was not just any group of parents. Willow Creek had a special ministry to children with physical and learning disabilities and to their parents. He was looking over notes for a banquet they gave each year especially in honor of the moms and dads who were raising children with special needs. He looked out the window of his office down onto the large lake that wrapped around the property and he could see children and some of the family fishing. He walked down to the water and when he got there he noticed quite a commotion going on just at the shore of the lake. One of the kids with Down Syndrome had caught her first fish. She was ecstatic. The parents were beside themselves seeing the joy of this little girl as she tried to drag this tiny fish out of the water.

He said he walked back up to his office to finish preparing for that night's banquet message. He remembered when they first raised the money to build that lake, getting permits, making plans, watching it fill up for the first time. Maybe all of that was just so this one little girl could catch her first fish. One little girl, one fish. Maybe that was the order from heaven.

God only knows.

Walking to the banquet room that night, he passed by a room where children of those parents were playing, watching DVDs, eating, and just being kids. No parents. Just a staff of trained workers and these special little kids. This was the one night that Willow Creek rolled out the red carpet to applaud the amazing effort of these parents, and to give them a night off. Just a night when they could enjoy an evening with each other and not worry about the safety and care of their children. It was their night.

Hybels said he looked into that room and saw the challenges of each child and wondered how tiring, how difficult at times, how lonely it might be to live out each day with these special needs kids. He walked into the banquet room to find it filled with parents of all ages and backgrounds, laughing, talking, eating and enjoying their night off. When he got up to speak, he looked into the eyes of men and women who looked tired. Some looked broken, and some looked like they didn't know how just to relax without their child in sight. He felt very inadequate to speak to this group of amazing parents, not having a child exactly like theirs. He said he did not want to be guilty of saying, "I know what you are going through," because he didn't. Reaching down as deep as he could, he finally told this group of parents,

"All I can say to you is this: Lean into God."

I remember that when he told that part of the story, during the evening service at Willow Creek, his voice cracked a bit. You could tell that, even though it had been many months since this banquet, it still moved him that these parents needed some level of hope.

Two ways to say everything.

"You know, if you just have enough faith Jesus will heal your son."

and

"All I can say to you is this: Lean into God."

One statement is full of arrogance and it deflates every ounce of hope and courage. The other is painfully honest by admitting, "I have nothing for you except the Lord; find shade under Him." It reminds me of when Job's three friends first found him sitting in sack cloth and ashes cutting himself with broken pieces of clay pottery. He had lost everything, except his wife who was telling him to curse God and die. He was at the bottom. His three friends showed up and the Bible says that they "said nothing, because there were no words adequate for the pain." Wow.

My friend did die. June 24, 2001. My son and his best friend were freshmen in high school and both had become close to this little boy. They played with him, ate with him, and watched movies with him, and so when he did die, his parents asked them both to be pall bearers at the funeral. I remember at the end of the service when the casket was being carried down the aisle of the church, my brother-in-law leaned over to me and said, "Our boys aren't 14 anymore; they became men today." It was true. I watched my son carrying that tiny casket down the aisle wondering what was going through his mind, how this would affect him. How much of this was he soaking up? I was proud of him that day. It was a day of so many emotions.

I did watch something happen from the first moment we found out he was sick with brain cancer. An entire group of adults caved in around that family. The prayer request first came during a large adult Bible study class one Sunday morning. When most of us who grew up in that town made the connection of who the little boy was, we realized we knew the dad from school. From that point on I saw people who otherwise may have never stepped out of their comfort zones make an effort to connect with a family that was hurting beyond words. I saw people who had never given actually empty their resources to help this family.

A benefit golf tournament drew in an entire community to raise money for the family and to send them on a dream vacation. I saw grown men weep when the huge cardboard check was given to the family. I saw men who had perfectly healthy kids at home give money like it was nothing. It was not about the money. It was not about the vacation. It was about allowing someone else's pain to become yours for one moment. That one moment can change you. I still hear from folks who mention that day or that year and how hard it was but how it affected them even to this day. I firmly believe that you and I most clearly reflect the heart of God when we reach out and lift someone up. As cheesy as that sounds, I really believe it. You look more like Christ when you are giving away what you have.

I remember sitting with my friend and his mom at the hospital one night when she told me the most amazing thing. I asked her how in the world she was coping with this pain and pending possible loss of her firstborn son. She said that God had given her peace at times when she felt so empty and helpless. She said she understood that if her son did die, most of the world would not stop for one moment on that day. Almost 100 percent of the world would move on as if nothing happened, even though her heart would be torn in half.

She said,

"I know the day he dies people will order ice cream all over the world. It's not that they don't care, it's just they never got to meet him. If they knew what a wonderful little boy he was, they would be sad too that he died, and they wouldn't be able to eat ice cream. They wouldn't be eating ice cream: they would be sad with me. But that's okay. My little boy loves ice cream."

What an incredible perspective.

Try this. Go to the store and buy some ice cream. I prefer Blue Bell Homemade Vanilla. Get some cups, spoons, napkins, and a cooler with some ice. Go to the local hospital in your town that has a pediatric cancer wing. Throw a party. Eat ice cream with those kids. Don't worry, the sugar is the least of their problems. Have fun. Sit on the floor and play a game with them. Learn their names. Meet their parents. Find the mom or dad that looks the most worn out and let them know you will be praying for them and for their child. Then leave. Go home and ask God to help those parents you just met lean into God.

Tuck your kids in bed.
Thank God for healthy kids and the kids with cancer.
Then thank Him for people around the world who are eating ice cream.

Every tomorrow has two handles. We
can take hold of it with the handle of
anxiety
or
the
handle
of faith.
Henry Ward Beecher

Every word of God is tried and purified;
He is a shield to those who trust and
take refuge in Him.
Proverbs 30:5 AMP

antique Bibles and unused train tickets.

I'm odd. Different. Unique. Some of my friends can come up with more colorful words than that. One of the odd things about me is I love to antique shop. I know, I know; get over it. Anyway, the reason I love to antique shop is that I really do enjoy finding things that are old and I love to imagine what it was like when folks first bought or used them. I love to find old books, and my favorite thing to antique shop for is old Bibles. Very old Bibles. My wife will tell you that she has lost me many times in the back of an antique shop on the floor going through stacks of old books and Bibles. I have Bibles dating back as far as 1689. I have lost a few bids on eBay for Bibles that are much older than this country.

Now for a confession. You might think the reason I like to collect old Bibles is that I am such a deeply spiritual person. Ha. Truth? The real reason is for what I sometimes find tucked in the pages. Stories have been told about very old stock certificates and land deeds found in the pages of old Bibles, which were sometimes the only safety deposit boxes before the turn of the century. Almost every one of the Bibles I have ever bought has had something tucked in the pages. No money, stocks, or land deeds though, yet.

One of my favorite antique Bibles is one I bought while on vacation years ago dated 1896. In the front of this Bible, written in pencil, is this simple inscription:

"Grace's first Bible."

Evidently the person who originally owned this Bible was
named Grace. But the most interesting thing I found tucked
away in the back of this Bible, buried in the pages of
First Timothy, was an unused train ticket for the Chicago
Reading Railroad dated "192_." Fascinating, isn't it?
Sometime during the 1920s, Grace or someone else,
bought a ticket on the Chicago Reading Railroad but never
used it.

Why?

Assuming Grace bought the ticket, was it just some
random, simple reason she never used it? Did she get
sick? Did she die? Did she place it in her Bible and then
forget it was there, missing her trip? How did that Bible end
up in a Texas antique shop, hundreds of miles away from
Chicago?

Here's a better question: Did Grace ever find grace? Did
Grace ever read the verse in Ephesians that says, "It is by
grace you have been saved . . ." Did she ever notice how
many times the word grace is used in the Bible, especially
in the New Testament? Did she ever, even just one time,
hear the voice of God say, "Grace, your name is the single
most important word to describe my love toward you." Did
she? Did someone sit her down and explain to her the
incredible meaning of her name?

Where was Grace going on the train? Was she running
from something? Was she running to something? Did
she ever find it? Why did God place Grace's Bible in my
hands? What was I supposed to learn from Grace's Bible?
What am I supposed to tell you about Grace's Bible? It
has been over 100 years since someone wrote, "Grace's
first Bible." I would imagine that Grace is most likely dead

today. Did she live life to the fullest? Did she ever find that verse in John 10:10 where Jesus said, "I have come that they would have life, and have it more abundantly." Did she grow old, marry, have children, and pass on to them what her name meant through the life and teachings of Christ found in the pages of that old Bible? Hopefully she did.

I have held that Bible before and wondered if she read verses or stories and then somehow connected the dots to God. I have also held that Bible in my hands and wondered what Grace looked like. How old was she when she first discovered the truth of that book? I have wondered what verses she missed. What story did she never read that might have unlocked a puzzle for her? Did she become a believer in Christ because of the teachings of that book? I have often tried to imagine what verses, if any, she took with her by memorizing a certain passage. Did she have a favorite story? Did she have a life verse tucked away in her heart that carried her through her life? What was the last thing she read?

Was this Bible with her when she died?

I wonder sometimes how much I know of who God is. Have I learned all of God that He intends me to learn? Have I learned any? What will I know of God on my last day on earth?

Have you ever thought about that? What if, on your last day on earth, you had 15 minutes to stop and think about how much of God, His word, and His people you had absorbed?

What did Grace know about God on her last day?

Is Grace's old Bible worn just because it is so old, or does it tell a story of a young woman who clung to that book for her very life? If I could sit down with Grace today and talk about her life, what story would she tell? I would love to see the look in her eyes when she told about what it was like in the 1920s and '30s when our nation was in the depth of a crippling depression, when most folks had no money, no job, and no hope. Would she be able to tell stories about reading passages of scripture in the Old Testament where, over and over again, the text would read,

". . . and God heard the cries of his children."

I imagine that if I could interview Grace she might say to me,

"We had nothing. We were so hungry most of time. I remember my family standing in bread lines for hours just to get enough food for one day or maybe one week. People were so tired. They were so sad. You could feel the heaviness in the air. No one dreamed. No one planned. It was pointless. All you could focus on was getting through the day. Survival. That was your main focus, just to survive. When I see pictures today of those years, they are always in black and white and at the time it seemed that way. No color, no life. Just black and white.

But our home was different.

We understood that even though times were so hard and it seemed as if there was no help in sight, God was still good. I remember my mother telling me,

'Grace, you must always seek the face of the Lord, not just His hand. Seek His face. Ask God to teach you what the verse means that says, "Seek the Lord while He may be found."'

Or she would say,

'Grace tonight before you go to bed, ask God to be with those who are less fortunate than we are. Thank Him for His blessings on our family; Grace, God is still good.' Somehow I knew then and certainly know now that it was in those moments I best learned and, because of those times, now understand the depth of God. I pressed in to Him on those cold nights when it seemed as if our family and our nation and even the world would collapse under the weight of that awful time. In those moments I could cry out to God and beg Him to send His cover and His peace to our home and our family. He did. He always did. Just when we thought we would not make another day, somehow we would be carried one more day. God is good, He is most surely good."

Maybe that is what Grace would tell me.

If someone were to buy your Bible 100 years from now in the back of an antique store, what would they find? What is your unused train ticket tucked away in the back somewhere? What are you running from or what are you running to? Why did you never use that ticket? What did you give up on? Where did your life end up? Where will mine end up?

If the pages of your Bible could talk, what would they say? Would they tell of the times when you lost yourself in the words of that book, only to find the hope or courage to battle one more day, one more disease, one more difficult child? If you buy my Bible, what falls out of it? What's my story?

Did I trust God?
Did I seek Him?
Did I know more of Him on my last day?
Did I love from a pure heart during the last month, last week, last day of my life?

Did Grace?
Did you?

You and I will place our hope and faith in something or someone. We will lean into something or someone for support. Even the most arrogant, disconnected atheist places their faith in the fact that they deeply believe there is no God. They lean into that; however empty that may be, they lean.

What are you leaning into?

I challenge you today to begin, or to continue, to lean into God. Regardless of how difficult or incredible your life and your day seem to be, lean into God. Someone, somewhere will find your "story," and they will draw from it a trace of where your hope came from. Leave a strong footprint. Make sure your path out of the cave leads them to hope and to help. Nothing is random, nothing is by chance. Grace's Bible did not just "happen" to end up in the back of that antique store.

Is it possible her life never made sense or mattered until you read this chapter?

If we have no peace, it is because we have forgotten that we belong to each other.
Mother Teresa

Jesus said to them, Fill the water pots with water. So they filled them up to the brim.
John 2:7 AMP

a glass of wine.

I am adding this chapter because I am a bit of a rebel. I really enjoy when someone colors outside the lines and gets results. I am not afraid anymore that someone will not like me because of what I say or who I support or I disagree with. I like a good argument when it helps clarify. We need more clarification. Life is a bit blurry sometimes.

I had a roommate at Baylor whose dad was my pastor when I was a child through the first grade. I remember sermons he preached; he was so practical and so easy to understand. I remember one time when he explained the holiness of God. He worked at a service station while he and his wife were dating, and he planned to take her to dinner one night after he got off work. After working all day at this gas station he went to the restroom and washed his hands. He scrubbed and scrubbed to get the dirt and grease off before they went to dinner. But when he jumped in his car to pick her up, to his horror he noticed his hands were still dirty. How did he miss it before? They looked so clean in the bathroom. What was the difference?

Sunlight.

The light in the bathroom was dim, but when he stepped out into the daylight, the dirt was exposed. I remember listening to the transition as he began to explain how that was just like our sin. As hard as we try and wash off the dirt from the day's sin, the man-made light of our lives never fully exposes what is left. We need a savior to wash us clean. All we need to do is walk out of the dark places where we are hiding, trying to wash what our hands have done, and step into the light of the Son. Once we have done that, He gladly takes us and washes away the guilt and stain of our sin. I got that. That made sense, even to a child. That picture was so simple to me that day. It was 1968 and I was six years old. I can still remember sitting on that wooden pew watching him paint that picture for me. It stuck.

It helped me connect the dots to God.

So, years later when I was standing at a mailbox in the dorm at Baylor, I noticed a side profile of someone I recognized. It was Wade, the son of my childhood pastor. My mom had been the church pianist and we had been childhood friends. I had not seen him in 15 years. Long story short, we became roommates that next year. It ended up being one of the most significant years of my life.

Baylor has this really cool marina. You can get sailboats and "sail" the Brazos River. I really don't know how much sailing is usually done on a river, but sail we did. One day Wade and I were out on a sailboat trying to sail on a windless Waco, Texas day. Not many Norman Rockwell scenes coming to mind, huh? Just two knuckleheads, trying to sail on a dead river with no wind. Yep, pretty goofy. Anyway, we could not figure out how to get that stupid sailboat to stay on course. We looked like a hockey puck, floating all over the Brazos. We ended up floating way down the river, farther and farther away from the dock. I have no idea how long we were out there.

Somewhere on the Brazos River, I asked Wade where he thought he might end up pastoring when he finished Baylor. Oh my gosh. I had no idea that question would begin a two-hour heated discussion. Just because his dad was a big-time pastor did not mean he had to do that too. He was going to be his own man. He was going to forge his own destiny. He was going to make his own way. He was going to march to a beat of a drummer that was not playing a pastor's beat. Maybe he would march to a plumber's beat or a carpenter's beat or an airline pilot's beat. Got the picture?

Now take a wild guess what drum beat Wade has been marching to for over 20 years? Oh yeah. You guessed it: a pastor. Big time. He is the head cook and bottle washer in Oklahoma. He was the president of the Oklahoma Baptist Convention. Number one dude of all the Baptists in the entire state of Oklahoma. And I get all the credit because I planted that seed in Wade's heart that afternoon on the Brazos River. Getting the Norman Rockwell feel yet? No? That's because I had nothing to do with Wade's drum beat!

I drag out that silly story for this point. Wade allowed God to use him to reach a family that speaks volumes to the butterfly effect of grace. Especially in light of the fact that he pastors a great church in a wonderful community that is Baptist. That is important. Very important. Part of the heritage of the Baptist church is their stance on alcohol. Not a drop. If you are Baptist, you don't drink alcohol. If you are Baptist and you do drink alcohol, you better not tell anyone. You know the joke: Baptists don't drink . . . in front of each other!

With permission from Wade, I share this story, straight from his blog site on the internet.

Years ago a man came into our services and sat through the preaching time weeping. He was a wealthy, high-profile business man who had just gone through a heart-wrenching divorce because of his own indiscretions.

After the service he introduced himself to me and set up an appointment to see me for some counseling. This began a six month pastoral relationship with this man that eventually led him to an understanding of the gospel of Jesus Christ and the ultimate experience of Divine forgiveness.

All that was now needed was reconciliation with his wife. He asked if I would counsel them. I said I would, but when he requested his wife to come with him to see me, she said, "No. He's a Baptist preacher. All he will do is condemn me." The businessman was crushed. I asked him why his wife was so hostile about Baptist preachers. He told me she grew up Roman Catholic and the only time she ever attended a Baptist Church the preacher yelled and screamed about the sins of the people in the pews including drinking, going to movies, wearing short skirts and long hair, etc . . . and it turned her off from "the Baptist religion."

I suggested that rather than have her come to my office that the man might want to see if his ex-wife (a divorce had since occurred) would have my wife and I over for dinner, just to get acquainted. To his surprise, she agreed. To our surprise she was a gourmet chef. We entered the lovely home with the smell of French bread wafting in the air, and sat at the table meticulously crafted for a true dining experience.

Unfortunately, though the introductions were cordial, I could tell the evening might be a long one because of the chill toward this "Baptist preacher." As we sat down, I noticed the brilliant table settings, the scrumptiously prepared French gourmet meal, and the solemn expression on the woman's face.

I also noticed there was tea and water on the table.

So this Baptist pastor said, "You can't have a meal like this without wine. Where is the wine?" I wish you could have seen her expression. She smiled and warmly said, "But I thought you were a Baptist preacher." "I am," was my response, "And this Baptist preacher knows a great chef when he sees one, and no chef worth her salt would prepare a meal like this without wine."

She asked my wife and me to follow her as she took us down to the cellar. She was a wine collector and she proudly showed us her collection, passed down to her by her grandfather. She meticulously chose a bottle of wine for the occasion and we made our way back to the table. I led us in prayer and we thanked God for the food and the drink and His provision for us. We ate a wonderful meal and I enjoyed a glass of wine. Nobody around the table had more than two glasses.

To make a long story short, the walls that had hindered the relationship came down. We enjoyed the evening with the couple and as a result five things happened:

(1). I was able to lead this woman to faith in Jesus Christ, showing her that Christ alone provided the righteousness she needed, and that she must forsake any trust in her own "self-righteousness." She trusted Him and was baptized shortly thereafter.

(2). It was my privilege to perform the private ceremony where wedding vows were exchanged again and this man and woman were reunited in marriage.

(3). The couple became very active in our church and have led out in our outreach of the lost in our community through Sunday School.

(4). They have personally given tens of thousands of dollars to the Lord's work through our church and Christian school, and have personally been able to lead several of their own family members to faith in Christ.

(5). They still have their wine collection, but have never been drunk since giving their lives to Christ as Lord.

Amazing? Not really. This woman and her husband had grace extended to them. I don't know this woman at all. I have never met her. How long had she stood at that bathroom sink trying over and over again to wash the grease off of her hands and get cleaned up for dinner? Someone needed to take her by the hand and walk her out into the light of the Son and allow Him to wash her. No, I have never met this woman, but I have met hundreds like her. Their story is the same. "They" don't fit in our clubs. "They" don't follow our rules. "They" don't deserve to sit in our section. They.

Let me tell you about "they."

They aren't polite anymore. They aren't sitting quietly on the back row, pretending to enjoy our games. They are done with our rules and our codes. They have decided to stay home and stay out of our churches. They are tired of trying to measure up, clean up, and straighten up. They have left the building. You can have your parking spot back. They're at home, where it's safe and familiar. Wouldn't you stay at home if you were them? I would.

Unless we extend the same grace that was given to us, the world will stay home and stay away from the good news of the gospel. The problem with most of the denominational church groups in the world is that they have forgotten why they exist. They exist to bring hope and help to a hurting and confused world. It really is that simple. They are the lighthouse in a raging storm in the middle of the night that has turned out the light because "that" ship doesn't play by the rules. They have a glass of wine on their deck. Turn the light off. Don't blow the horn. They would be better off crashing into the rocks than spilling their sin on our shore.

Think I'm exaggerating?

Ask anyone. Ask anyone why they don't attend a local church anymore. Listen to their answers and don't judge. Don't let yourself get away with a cheap reason like, "They're just sinners. That's what sinners do." No. No. No. No. Our message seems not to be good news anymore and they have cast their vote of "not interested." Good news is still good news.

This woman in Wade's blog is real. She really did not know God loved her unconditionally. She really did not know how to mend her broken life and marriage. She did not think those people down at the local church cared. Worse, she most likely knew they would judge her because she had a wine cellar.

Watch that story unfold from the view of heaven. Did we almost cash in a woman's life for a glass of wine? How many Baptist pastors would have sat at that table and drank one glass of wine to share the love of God with that woman? 100 percent of zero? God help us. Please God, help us!

The first public miracle Jesus performed was turning water into wine. The disciples came to Him and told Him they were out of wine. Why didn't He say, "Good, I hate that stuff. Makes me dizzy, and gives me a headache. I'm glad they ran out. It will send you to hell anyway. Everyone at this wedding is going straight to hell!" No, He didn't, did He? He had the servants bring Him barrels of water and He turned it to wine.

He turned the water into wine.

Think about that. What are we missing, besides buckets and buckets of grace? We're missing common sense. The entire issue of alcohol is control. The Bible clearly teaches that anything that controls me—food, money, wine, anything—is wrong. Anything in my life that takes control, other than the Spirit and heart of God, is wrong, because it becomes an idol that my soul will worship. So if wine is the central focus of my life, it is wrong. The draw of the Lordship of Christ is that I follow His life and teaching, in everything. Anything that blocks that ultimately destroys my life.

I am so glad that Wade and Rachel went to this lady's house, ate dinner, and drank a glass of wine. It was a good year. It was a very good year. I would imagine the bottle of wine that was brought up from the cellar had been there for years. The grapes were carefully grown, picked, crushed, fermented, and then bottled. When she bought that bottle of wine, she had no idea how it would change her life. Can you imagine if the person who took her money handed her the bottle and said,

"Just think, someday after you go through a painful divorce, the local Baptist preacher and his wife will open this bottle with you, share a glass, and you will find the love of God in a way you never imagined. You'll be reconciled with the Lord and with your husband. You'll be remarried, and your family will be restored. You will find a new life in the work of the kingdom of God. Just like He turned this grape juice into wine, He will transform your life as well. Enjoy!"

I love that story. It is a perfect picture of what can and does happen when you and I put down our agendas and offer mercy and grace to a desperate world. The point of this story is not wine, or alcohol, or Baptist preachers, or whether drinking is bad or good. The point of this story is that people need to know that they still matter to God. They need to know that there is hope outside the walls of their lives. They need to hear you and me tell them they can start over. They need to know that nothing they could ever do, good or bad, could cause the heart of God to love them any more or less than He does right now. They need grace.

Remember when I mentioned that Wade and I floated the Brazos River like a hockey puck? Were you curious why we weren't cutting across the water like a good sail boat should? It's because we were sitting on the rudder, the thing that gives you the ability to, well, not just float aimlessly. We were rudderless. No way to steer across the water. No matter how hard we tried, we could not go the way we wanted. Something was missing. But it was right there all the time. We just kept floating down the river. Other sail boats were cutting back and forth across the river. It was as if they knew something we didn't. It would have been nice if they would have come over to us and showed us how to use the rudder for something other than a bench. We didn't know. Someone needed to show us.

We were not bad people; we just didn't know. We were lost and confused.

It would have made all the difference in the world that day.

You never know God is all you need
until
God is all you have.
Rick Warren

"Come and meet a man who told me
everything I ever did! Can this be the
Messiah?"
So the people came
streaming
from the village to see him.
John 4:29-30 NLT

an empty water bucket.

It was a day when I felt like stories in the Bible, especially in the New Testament, seemed to be different, seemed to be real. Not in a weird way, just a very different way. For the first time I saw the stories in the New Testament as if they happened last night, not two thousand years ago. Real people, real conversations, real pain, real joy, real death. Real. Something different played in my mind's eye when I pictured Jesus walking, talking, or just sitting as He watched people.

It happened when I was reading in John 4, where Jesus meets the person you and I call "the woman at the well." Pick up a Bible and read that story. Picture Jesus as He walks up to the well. Remember, He knows every word that is about to be exchanged with this obscure woman who is an absolute outcast in her world. He walks up to the well, and this sentence falls off the page:

"And Jesus, tired from the journey, sits down."

There it is. One of the most amazing sentences in the New Testament. Go with me for a minute. I've tried to imagine how the Gospels were put together. Did someone literally stand next to Jesus all day and night and "record" what was said and done? Maybe, maybe not. What if at the end of a long day one of the disciples sat down next to Jesus and began to write as he thought back through that day's journey? Maybe Jesus would say something as simple as, "John, write this down" or, "Did you get that?" However it was recorded, I have to imagine it was amazing for the disciples to watch as Jesus opened up His life to them, knowing they were writing down what He was saying and doing among the people.

On this occasion, in John 4, Jesus must have retold the conversation of meeting this woman. He probably said to His disciples, "I was tired, so I sat down next to the well where she was drawing water." Do you think that the other disciples looked at each other? What was going through their minds? At least one of the disciples or maybe all of them, must have thought, "Jesus got tired? Did He just say 'tired'? I know I just heard Him say He was tired. Is that possible? I got tired today, too. I had no idea He knew what it was like to get tired and need to rest!"

Can you imagine if you were one of the twelve and you begin to notice that the same guy who could walk on water and drive out demons got tired and needed to sit down and rest? Right after He raised that little girl from the dead, maybe He turned around and said,

"I'm hungry. You guys hungry? Let's get something to eat."

I don't know about you but that helps me. Maybe, as much as I need a carving of Jesus on a cross, I need a carving of Him sitting on a rock with the inscription underneath:

"And Jesus, tired from the journey, sat down."

I do need the crucifixion, but I need to be reminded I can identify with Christ in every area of my life. Especially when I am tired and need to rest.

I believe Christ was the creator of the entire universe. I really do. I know in my heart He controls everything. He called the worlds into existence. I believe that. What is hard sometimes is to remember that when I am depressed, lonely, frustrated, or angry, I can and I should go to Him. He is still my great high priest who understands everything about me. I will never shock or disappoint Him.

Back to the well.

Jesus got tired and He sat down. Notice when He got tired He didn't keep going, keep walking, and keep pushing. He sat down. He sat down because He was tired, but He also sat down and rested because He needed to demonstrate to the woman at the well that it was ok to be worn out. He knew, among many other things, that she needed a God that could take a break and rest. The great news about Jesus is that He sees right through to the heart. This is not a surface god. This is Jesus.

The encounter with this woman is so important to you and me. I think this is one of the most significant chapters in the entire Bible. Of all the powerful, mystical moments in the New Testament, this one stands out for me. The drama and dialogue in the fourth chapter of John is one of my favorites at so many levels. This story sets the foundation for the direction and the divinity of the life and teaching of Christ. More than any other story of the New Testament, this launches who Jesus is. Look closely. Notice the words that are exchanged. This is a one-on-one dialogue between Jesus and this unnamed woman. And remember that at the moment this conversation took place, she was the most unlikely candidate to be placed front and center for a teaching moment from scripture.

No one came to her that morning and said, "Put on something different. Blue. Blue is your color. Now this is important, so smile a lot. This is the son of God. He's

Jewish, but it's okay. Relax, and also, He knows everything about you. Yes, He knows that too. Calm down, it's going to be okay; you're going to be famous. They'll teach about you in seminary classes and churches all over the world someday. You will now be known as 'the woman at the well.' Aren't you glad He isn't meeting you at a barn? Anyway, just be yourself. I hear he's very nice. You'll do fine."

It didn't happen that way. She was doing what she does every day at this time. This day was just like every other day. Lonely. Empty. Regretful. Shallow. Uneventful. For those of you who will allow me to stretch and bend your theology, maybe she hadn't prayed in years. Maybe she was not expecting anything wonderful, powerful, or life changing. What if this was not an answer to prayer? Maybe God chose to redirect this woman's compass because He is God. It was time. Maybe that morning Jesus asked His Father to send the most desperate soul to Him.

Maybe this side of heaven, it was just that simple.

It is easy for me to forget how outcast and empty this woman was. So much of who she was, and more importantly who she wasn't, is laid out in the text. Jesus went out of His way to meet this woman.

I love the fact that Jesus kept turning her responses back to her pain and to her emptiness. Every time she would respond to His comment or to His question, He would push her back to the place of her deepest need. Read John 4. Now read it again. And now read it out loud. Then read it to someone else and then ask them what picture they have in their mind at the end of the chapter.

The dialogue between Jesus and the woman ends in a powerful moment when Jesus turns to her and says in verse twenty-one:

"Believe me, woman, a time is coming when you will worship the Father neither on this mountain nor in Jerusalem. You Samaritans worship what you do not know; we worship what we do know, for salvation is from the Jews." (NIV)

Salvation is from the Jews?

"Excuse me," the world says.

You really don't have to stretch to think how odd that was. Imagine the leader of Israel calling a press conference today. Cameras are pointed at one podium. Backdrop is that light blue flag with the Star of David in the middle. He begins to speak and after a few sentences you hear this:

"We are fast approaching a time when the entire world, who does not worship the correct god, will follow the Jews and worship our God. The salvation of the world will come from the Jews."

Just imagine that.

What Jesus proposed was much, much more radical. When Jesus told the Samaritan woman that genuine worship would no longer be done like tradition said it should, but it would be done from the heart, He train-wrecked the system. Real worship would be forever changed, and the history of that little nation would forever change. Jesus divided time. As much as we see BC vs. AD, you could almost make a case that this audience of one, unnamed, would begin part two of history. Jesus made His announcement to a societal outcast that everything would be different.

Equally amazing is the last part of that exchange when Jesus says,

"Yet a time is coming and has now come when the true worshipers will worship the Father in spirit and truth, for they are the kind of worshipers the Father seeks. God is spirit, and his worshipers must worship in spirit and in truth." (NIV)

I have always wondered what exactly Jesus meant. "A time is coming *and has now come. . .*" Was that it? Did the change occur during His sentence? Did the change happen, somewhere deep in the corner of the heavens, right then? When Jesus said, "Yet a time is coming," did the Father stand up and give the command? Had God been waiting for that sentence to be spoken? You may say, "Come on. Lighten up!"

Hold on.

If you were God, how long would you have been ready for your children to stop trying to gain your forgiveness and affection? How many chapters of Leviticus could you stand to see performed over and over again? How many lambs could you watch be slaughtered? You as God knew better than anyone that this system of sin, sacrifice, sin, sacrifice, sin, sacrifice did not work. It did not atone for the sins of the people. It did not appease the justice and wrath of a God who is so holy that sin cannot be in His presence.

Understand that Jesus was saying to the woman at the well that day, "I have to die, or you will never have peace. You will never experience real joy. If I don't go to the cross, you will spend the rest of your life clawing your way up a hill only to find another, and another, and another. It's work you will never complete. It will only bore out a deeper hole in your heart. Your effort is worthless. Your religion is void. Your day is futile. Because of that, I will rescue you."

This woman didn't need a marriage counselor. She didn't need a match maker. She didn't need therapy. She needed the deepest part of her soul to be healed.

So do you.
So do I.

She needed Jesus to step inside her heart and write:

You are not a mistake.
You are not worthless.
You are not trash.
You are not used up.

You are a daughter of the King.
Your best days are ahead of you.
They are wrong.
Trust me.
Jump. I will catch you.

When I think about the woman at the well, I remember a scene in *The Passion of the Christ* that stood out more than others for me. Jesus is carrying the cross to Calvary on a narrow, cobblestoned street when He falls down and the weight of the cross comes crushing down on top of him. As Mary, His mother, is running toward Him, she flashes back to picking Him up as a little boy. Do you remember? Just as she bends down to Jesus, by now almost unrecognizable from the beatings, He turns to her and says something.

Do you remember what He says?

"See, Mother, I make all things new."

O my soul. I realize Gibson took liberties to add scenes and lines like that, but it felt right. That is what Jesus did that day. It was the reason for all that blood. For all that pain. For all that torture. It was why you almost came out of your seat when they kept beating Him with that whip. It was the reason for every second of His thirty-three years on earth. It balanced all of Heaven. In II Corinthians 5:17, Paul says it this way: "If anyone is in Christ, he is a new creation. Old things have passed away, behold all things become new." The phrase "new creation" literally translates, "a species of being that has never existed before."

The result? All things become new.
All things.
Not some things.
Not most things.
Not almost everything.
All things.
All things become what?
New.

This woman, who had been passed around town by five different men, had to be the joke of her community. This last guy just moved in. No marriage. No ring. No party. Just sit your shoes over there. Hang your coat here.

Wipe your feet on my heart. Go ahead; everyone else has. No wonder this woman ran back into her little village and compelled the entire town to follow her back to meet Jesus. She knew something was different. She knew this wasn't just any prophet. She had seen prophets. She had heard prophets. This man was different. How did she do it? How did she get the entire village to follow her back to Christ? What was her system? What was her training? How did she phrase the right question?

Watch this.

"Come meet a man who told me everything I ever did! Can this be the Messiah?" So the people came streaming from the village to see him.

Streaming?

How perfect. Do you think this poor woman understood what she was saying? Everyone in town already knew her life story. How in the world could you be married and divorced five times and it not be everyone's whisper? You're not the rumor; you are the story. More than one person had to think,

"I could have done that. I could tell her everything she ever did. We all know her story!"

Somehow her delivery was different. There had to be a glow about her that said, "Come meet a man who told me everything I ever did—and He loved me anyway. He forgave me in spite of that. He gave me hope. He can give you hope too. Come back with me. Please. There has got to be more to life than this."

What if He is the one?
What if this is the Messiah we have been waiting for?
What if I am wrong?

So the people came streaming from the village to see him. Mission accomplished. The goal that day was not to convert the entire planet. Most of the world ignored, rejected, or scoffed at the message of Christ. But this woman and this village needed hope and needed saving, needed a new story, needed a new beginning. The water in that well didn't need to be filtered. It needed to be replaced. Jesus dug a new well. He filled it with living water.

When I think about the woman at the well and the streaming line of people chasing after Jesus, I get a picture of the crowd gathered around listening to Jesus, soaking up this amazing man. Just imagine this woman, worn out from the emotion of the day, standing or maybe sitting to the side. Not a part of the pressing throngs. She is back to being invisible. Her fifteen minutes of fame is over. All of a sudden, at the end of His teaching time, Jesus calls out her name. Everyone is hushed, amazed that He knows her name and even more amazed that He seems to be looking for her. The crowd parts as Jesus sees her at the back, sitting down leaning against a tree. Startled, she realizes Jesus and all eyes are focused on her. He motions toward her and says,

Tomorrow?
Noon?
Water?

Maybe, just maybe, Jesus walks away from the crowd and the woman and joins His disciples. He looks over at Mary, puts His arm around her, leans in, and whispers,

"See, Mother, I make all things new."

grace.

I want to end with this challenge.

Look for opportunities to cause a butterfly effect of grace.

Think differently.
Act differently.
See people differently.

See them the way Christ saw them. Stop measuring your life in how comfortable you can be. Become a giver. Not only of your time and your resources, but become a giver of your life. Give your life away. Make a soft place for someone else to land. Never forget how difficult life is for almost everyone else in the world.

Almost everyone else in the world tonight.

If I had one prayer for this book it would be that you would see others in a new light. If you and I see people for who they could be, should be, and might become, we might be more accepting of their rough edges.

Their dirt and dogs will not bother us so much.

Think about this. Galatians Chapter 5, verse 22-23 is a nine-word list of the 'produce' that will fall off the vine when God plants His Spirit inside of you and I. One of the words in that list that seems odd is kindness. Verse 22 says, "The fruit of the Spirit is love, joy, peace, patience, kindness, goodness, faithfulness, gentleness and self-control." From the NIV, it is literally right in the middle of the list. Four on either side. It's not first or last, just hiding in the middle.

Kindness.

If there was a verse that just may sum up the butterfly effect of grace, it is Galatians 5:22-23. And if there were a word that describes the one act that will always open that door, it would be kindness. It feels sometimes like we have lost the art of being kind. It seems we are too busy or in a hurry to stop and think that a kind word or act may be the most significant thing we do that day.

It sounds almost lame in a world that is so driven on power, success, and speed, that something as basic as putting the other person's needs above your own could really make a difference.

I believe it could.

As a friend of mine says, live intentionally. Pay attention to the world right at your feet. Begin to listen and watch how often it seems we live within touching distance of people who are so bruised and broken. I know it isn't always true, but it really does feel like we don't care. I promise you the people we ignore and walk past think we don't care. Reaching out to someone who is hurting, discouraged, or lonely is the very heartbeat of Christ.

It changes the world by changing their world.

Ask yourself this question, who am I supposed to impact today? It is almost never the extravagant that changes someone's life. You will connect the dots to God for someone else by simply extending a hand up, not just a hand out. Some of the most profound moments in my life have been when someone took the time to write a note or say something directly to me.

I remember that.
I felt that.
It mattered.

It will matter to them too.

This book is about the moments when something was done or said to another person, many times in a very simple way that impacted them. Hopefully it caused them to extend that same grace to others. It moved the ocean in their world and caused a ripple effect. This isn't just another version of pay it forward. This is about you and I getting in the flow of what God may be doing to recapture the heart and affection of someone by using your life. Your words. Your hands.

Remember, this is not your home. What happened today, last week, last year, is not the end. In fact, in the scope of all eternity, it is a microscopic dot in an endless line of time. But that dot is significant. It is significant because it falls from a sovereign plan for a loving Father to gather back to Himself a lost, scattered people.

That's all.

So, what now?

Live your life. Raise your families. Work your jobs. Coach little league baseball. Travel. Cook. Eat. Play. Rest. Grow old and then die. Along the way, fall head over heels in love with the God of the universe who chased you down and gave you His word and His Son.

Find the Kingdom of God. It is happening all around you.

Seek it first, above everything else in your life, seek it first. And in doing that you will discover a journey filled with joy, pain, love, heartbreak, adventure, suffering, and life. Life to the fullest. Be careful to watch for hitchhikers who have lost their way, need a lift, and need to get home. Teach them how to do the same by the kindness you show them. If you and I do a better job of that, I believe, it will cause a butterfly effect of grace.

If you would like to find out more about this book, the Butterfly Effect of Grace, or more about the author, Rex Russell, join us at www.butterflyeffectofgrace.com

Again, may you discover the endless ways to create a butterfly effect of grace in the world today. Share your story with us at the site listed above. We look forward to walking with you in this new awareness of grace.

rest in Him,
rex

CPSIA information can be obtained
at www.ICGtesting.com
Printed in the USA
BVHW071418120620
581230BV00004B/161

9 781606 471937